Helping Adolescents and Adults to Build Self-Esteem

of related interest

Helping Children to Build Self-Esteem
Deborah Plummer
ISBN 1 85302 927 0

**Relationship Development Intervention: with Young Children
and with Children, Adolescents and Adults**
**Social and Emotional Development Activities for Asperger Syndrome,
Autism, PDD and NLD**
Steven E. Gutstein and Rachelle K. Sheely
ISBN 1 84310 720 1 (2 volume set)

Using Interactive Imagework with Children
Walking on the Magic Mountain
Deborah Plummer
ISBN 1 85302 671 9

Helping Adolescents and Adults to Build Self-Esteem

A Photocopiable Resource Book

Deborah Plummer

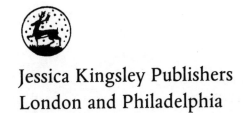

Jessica Kingsley Publishers
London and Philadelphia

Material on activity sheets 5.1, 8.1, 8.8 and 8.10 and Appendix A adapted with permission from *You Can Change – A Self-help Guide to Managing Stress* (2003) by Diane Eaglen and Deborah Plummer.
© Adult Speech and Language Therapy Service 2003.

First published in 2005 by
Jessica Kingsley Publishers
116 Pentonville Road
London N1 9JB, UK
and
400 Market Street, Suite 400
Philadelphia, PA 19106, USA

www.jkp.com

Reprinted twice in 2005
Fourth impression 2006

Library of Congress Cataloging in Publication Data
Plummer, Deborah.
 Helping adolescents and adults to build self-esteem : a photocopiable resource book /
Deborah Plummer.— 1st American pbk. ed.
  p. cm.
 Includes bibliographical references and index.
 ISBN 1-84310-185-8 (pbk.)
 1. Self-esteem in adolescence. 2. Self-esteem. I. Title.
 BF724.3.S36P55 2004
 155.2'5—dc22

2004020235

British Library Cataloguing in Publication Data
A CIP catalogue record for this book is available from the British Library

ISBN-13: 978 1 84310 185 7
ISBN-10: 1 84310 185 8

Printed and Bound in Great Britain by
Athenaeum Press, Gateshead, Tyne and Wear

Contents

Part III: Information and Activity Sheets

Acknowledgements

I am grateful to all the members of groups that I have had the privilege of facilitating during my years of working in the NHS. I learned a great deal about the diversity of groups and the pitfalls and joys of group work during this time (and I am, thankfully, continuing to learn!).

I am also grateful to Dr Dina Glouberman and my Imagework colleagues, particularly Hermione Elliott and Marsha Lomond, who have taught me so much about group facilitation by being such inspirational facilitators themselves.

My family, who have always endeavoured to support my self-esteem, have been particularly patient and supportive while I have been writing – providing words of encouragement, constructive feedback and welcome diversions!

Introduction

To hold someone in high esteem is to respect and admire them. When we respect and admire someone we accord them value – we appreciate, cherish, hold dear. What a tragedy that so many people are unable to do this for themselves – to cherish and appreciate their own worth; to value themselves for who they are. Self-esteem is talked about and written about in great depth, but for many the ability to achieve a healthy level of self-esteem seems perpetually elusive. Since the way that a person feels about himself to a large extent determines the way he behaves, learns and relates to other people, low self-esteem can have far-reaching and debilitating effects in all arenas of life.

Fortunately, there is much that can be done to build and maintain self-esteem.

> Since the feeling of worth has been learned, it can be unlearned, and something new can be learned in its place. The possibility for this learning lasts from birth to death, so it is never too late. At any point in a person's life he can begin to feel better about himself. (Satir 1991, p.27)

This book offers a variety of ways to help others to build self-esteem, primarily through facilitating the process of understanding and changing unwanted patterns of thinking and behaviour in order to create new ways of facing life's challenges. It is based on the premise that low self-esteem is not a discrete issue that can be addressed with specific 'feel good about yourself' activities alone. Rather, it is based on the strengthening of seven vital 'foundation' elements. Healthy self-esteem cannot be separated from these elements, but instead should be seen as potentially the *end result* of addressing them.

Readers who have already come across my earlier book *Helping Children to Build Self-Esteem* will be familiar with the format used here. However, I have expanded on the theoretical component and, in particular, I have devoted a complete section to exploration of the skills needed to facilitate groups and to understand group processes.

Once again the photocopiable information and activity sheets can be used as a complete course or as a resource to dip into and adapt as needed. Whilst emphasis has been given to group work, the majority of the information and activity sheets are suitable for use in a wide range of educational and therapeutic settings. They are equally appropriate for work with individual clients or pupils, particularly where there is opportunity for structured support to aid the transfer of skills and strategies to a variety of situations relevant to that person's life.

Please note that throughout the text the pronouns 'he' and 'she' have been used interchangeably.

Suggestions for further reading

Glouberman, D. (2003) *Life Choices, Life Changes: Develop Your Personal Vision with Imagework.* London: Hodder and Stoughton.

Plummer, D. (1999) *Using Interactive Imagework with Children: Walking on the Magic Mountain.* London: Jessica Kingsley Publishers.

Plummer, D. (2001) *Helping Children to Build Self-Esteem.* London: Jessica Kingsley Publishers.

Part I

Theoretical and Practical Background

Chapter 1

What Is Self-Esteem?

Attempting to help others to build self-esteem without due reference to which specific *aspect* of self-esteem a person is struggling with can be in-effective and may actually do harm. For example, encouraging someone to feel positive about herself without helping her to build competency skills in the area she is working on could lead her to try things before she is ready and therefore set herself up for failure. Helping others to build self-esteem is also about helping them to 'get along in the world': it involves taking into account the personal and social context in which each individual operates.

It is therefore vital for facilitators to have an understanding of what self-esteem is all about and to be able to use this understanding to inform the way that they structure their support.

The link between self-concept and self-esteem

Our *self-concept* is the overall view that we have of ourselves. This includes our appearance, ability, temperament, attitudes and beliefs.

This overall view is heavily influenced by the way in which we interpret 'feedback messages' from other people – the way we perceive their reactions to what we do and say – and this process begins with our earliest interactions as babies.

Generally, we try to act in a way that fits in with our self-concept. This means that when new information is received to add to our system of beliefs about ourselves, we are likely to 'filter out' the bits that we think are not relevant to us. If the information fits in with our self-concept, we will probably accept it as being true (even if it is not based on any factual evidence). If it is not consistent with how we see ourselves, then we might ignore it, misinterpret it or reject it completely. In this way our beliefs affect the way we see the world and this, in turn, informs our behaviour.

Healthy self-esteem or 'positive self-regard' is about feeling competent *and* feeling lovable or 'approved' of. It involves the *evaluation* of the self-concept and is often unrelated to our true abilities. We can have different levels of self-esteem in different areas of our lives. The extent to which self-esteem in these different 'domains' affects our global sense of self-worth will depend on the level of importance we place on each domain.

The nature of a child's self-evaluations appears to change markedly from early to late childhood. Very young children tend to think of themselves in terms of absolutes. Their self-evaluations usually involve descriptions of behaviours, abilities and preferences and are often unrealistically positive. They are not yet able to compare their competencies with those of others in a realistic way. However, even young children can demonstrate low self-esteem if their life experience has emphasized negative attributes (Harter 1999).

The difference between the perceived self (self-concept) and the 'ideal' self gives an indication of self-esteem. If a person's view of herself is close to how she would like to be, then she can be said to have healthy self-esteem. 'Ideal' doesn't have to equate with 'perfect', but someone with low self-esteem may well create unrealistic concepts of how she would like to be, or how she thinks she 'should' be.

As young children we rely heavily on external means to confirm our self-worth and competence. We look to the significant people in our lives (parents, grandparents, teachers, etc.) to show us that we are loved and approved of. Virginia Satir, family therapist, writes:

> An infant coming into the world has no past, no experience in handling himself, no scale on which to judge his own worth. He must rely on the experiences he has with the people around him and the messages they give him about his worth as a person. (Satir 1991, p.24)

The way that we interpret verbal and non-verbal messages from others plays an important part in this. By non-verbal I mean such aspects as facial expression, body language and even the structure of our environment. Healthy self-esteem is most easily built up when input from others is accepting, non-judgemental and unambiguous.

> The infant needs to be able to discover his/her capacity to light up the mother's face – for here is to be found the fundamental basis of...self-esteem. (Casement 1990, p.93)

If a child's early experiences have been primarily positive with regard to the building of self-esteem, then eventually he will be able to internalize the feelings of self-worth and rely less and less on others for approval and confirmation that he is OK. However, a child who remains dependent on external sources for the maintenance of self-esteem will find life's difficulties harder to handle since he will invariably use the actions and reactions of other people to define himself.

> Such a child will develop into an adult who will continue to feel that he has to be successful, or good, or approved of by everyone, if he is to retain any sense of his own value. (Storr 1989, p.96)

There are also indications that patterns of interaction in early childhood affect the developing brain. Research neuroscientist Lise Eliot, for example, cites a study undertaken by researchers at the University of Washington who compared frontal-lobe EEG measures in the infants of depressed and non-depressed mothers. They found that by about one year of age, babies whose mothers were depressed showed a different pattern of neural responsiveness than control babies. During playful interactions they experienced less activation of the left hemisphere (the 'feel-good' side) than control babies (Eliot 1999).

So, chronic low self-esteem may be a product of childhood experiences and belief patterns, but feelings of self-worth and competency can also be affected when we are feeling particularly vulnerable, for example after loss of a loved one, change in work circumstances, redundancy or long-term illness. For some people, such changes affect the way that they have always defined themselves in life, the roles they have played (partner, parent, provider, decision-maker, expert, etc.), and with this loss or blurring of roles comes a loss of self-esteem. Whilst most of us would be affected to some degree by these changes, for those who have little or no internal self-esteem resources such events can result in a debilitating, disabling period of depression from which it is difficult to break free.

Adolescence and self-esteem

Self-esteem can also be affected as we move from one stage of life to another. For example, moving from being dependent on our parents to finding out who we are and where we fit into the world; starting a family of our own; entering the renowned 'mid-life' period; reaching old age, when our roles may be changing yet again.

Adolescence, and the physical, emotional and mental changes that accompany this tumultuous time, can often herald a period of great uncertainty and vulnerability. Young adolescents may be mourning the passing of childhood, however much they may want to be more 'grown up'. This period is often marked by a feeling of loss of self and an epic struggle to re-invent or rediscover the 'real' self.

Part of this process may involve the young adolescent deliberately alienating others, particularly family; pushing them away 'to see what is left'. It is a time when peers become increasingly important and play a vital role in helping the adolescent to define himself and to build his self-esteem as an independent person. At the same time, although he may crave independence, he is also grappling with the need for nurture and friendship. He is full of doubts about his acceptability to others, about where he 'fits in' to the greater scheme of life, about his body and about the reality of his thoughts.

The link between low self-esteem and adolescent suicides has been explored by several researchers. For example, in a study involving adolescent psychiatric in-patients and high-school students Overholser and colleagues concluded that low self-esteem was closely related to higher levels of depression, hopelessness and suicidal ideation, and an increased likelihood of having previously attempted suicide (Overholser *et al.* 1995). Low self-esteem has also been linked to adolescent use and abuse of alcohol and drugs, adolescent pregnancy and unprotected sexual encounters (e.g. California Task Force to Promote Self-Esteem and Personal and Social Responsibility 1990; Harper and Marshall 1991).

Eric Rayner refers to adolescence as a process of transition which may be quiet and enjoyable for some but is nevertheless a period of 'crisis' for most:

A life crisis is a personal situation which arises when well-tried structures of adaptation and defence are no longer adequate to assimilate new demands, which may impinge either from within or from outside the individual. Loosening up with at least partial disintegration of thought and feeling then occurs. This is accompanied by anxiety and perplexity and often also impulsive action. (Rayner 1993, p.141)

Rayner goes on to say that the adolescent is 'a bundle of fantasies of possibilities'.

He is not yet someone with a set appearance or with an identity which has been tested in the society around him… As the sense of self is so much at the centre of questions for the adolescent, it is no wonder that he makes it a focus of preoccupation. (Rayner 1993, p.157)

This process of transition may continue beyond the years of adolescence and into adulthood in one form or another.

Maslow's view of self-esteem

Abraham Maslow, one of the founders of humanistic psychology, noted that some needs in our lives take precedence over others. For example, the basic needs of water and food take precedence over the need for shelter. He formulated a 'hierarchy of needs' that can be represented in the form of a pyramid (Maslow 1954):

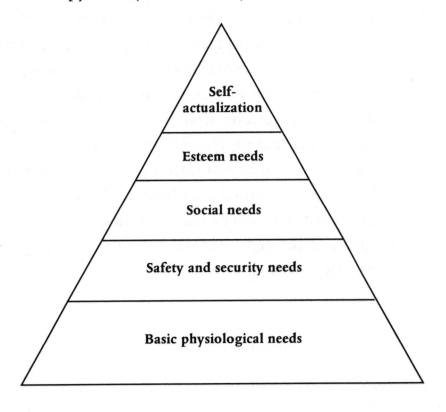

Maslow argued that only when the needs at the base of the pyramid were for the most part satisfied could those higher up be addressed. So, when physiological and safety needs are taken care of - you have enough to satisfy your basic living needs – you begin to feel the need for friends and family or to seek a sense of being part of a community. Beyond this Maslow identified two types of esteem needs. The lower one he described as the need for the respect of others, the need for status, recognition, and so on. The higher form relates to the need for self-respect, which includes feelings of confidence and competence.

For the majority of us, our basic needs in this hierarchy are fulfilled to some degree. However, it is often at the level of esteem that we struggle. Maslow saw all these needs, including self-esteem, as survival needs. He argued that self-esteem is necessary for well-being and that, like needs lower down in the pyramid, the need for esteem is genetically a part of us.

At the top of the pyramid, Maslow placed 'self-actualization' – the ability to become truly 'me' and to fulfil my potential. Maslow in fact had quite a narrow view of what self-actualization meant and proposed that only a very small percentage of us would ever reach the stage of being fully self-actualized. He talked of a constant conflict between our need for growth and development and our need for safety and stability. When we are concerned primarily with the latter then we will tend not to take chances or try out new things; but when our lower needs are reasonably catered for we are more likely to risk stepping into the unknown in order to promote our general development. This is not an absolute, however. Sometimes it is dissatisfaction with the needs lower down the hierarchy that provides the driving force to activate the higher ones. However, if we follow his argument in general principle, it would hold that people with low self-esteem are highly unlikely to reach, or even to be motivated to seek, self-actualization. Furthermore, for those of us who do not have our basic needs met, it will be these basic needs that will be our motivating factors in life and that must be addressed before we can reach the stage of recognizing and building our self-esteem.

What happens if self-esteem is low?

People with low self-esteem will invariably have problems in forming close attachments, partly because it is often so difficult for them to believe themselves worthy of a fulfilling relationship with another person. Low self-esteem can also lead to anxiety and confusion where misunderstandings can easily occur and where there is a tendency to do a lot more biased 'filtering' (see p.14), leading to a distorted view of self and others. People who have low self-esteem may act in a very passive way or may be aggressive, quick to get in first before they themselves are attacked, rejecting others before they are rejected.

> To defend themselves, they hide behind a wall of distrust and sink into the terrible human state of loneliness and isolation. (Satir 1991, p.22)

They tend to place little value on their abilities and often deny their successes. They find it difficult to set goals and to problem-solve. Self-confidence is reduced and there is an unwillingness to try because of fear of failure. Consequently, they may perform well below their academic and social capabilities. They invariably begin to expect the worst in life and their self-limiting beliefs become a self-fulfilling prophecy.

There are also many people who *do* achieve at or near their academic potential but have a constant fear of failure and a drive for perfection that may preclude creativity and experimentation. Such a person may set unrealistically high goals for himself, thus constantly confirming to himself that he is 'no good' each time that he experiences failure.

The benefits of healthy self-esteem

Helping someone to build self-esteem is not the same as encouraging a reluctant acceptance of 'this is who I am'. Nor is it necessarily the same as encouraging someone to strive for 'self-actualization' as Maslow defined it. The opposite of low self-esteem might simply be 'a quiet pleasure in being one's self' (Rogers 1961, p.87). This alone can have huge implications for the way that someone might lead his life.

A person who believes in himself and who has developed a degree of self-reliance is more likely to be able to cope with life's inevitable difficulties and failures. He will be able to weather the occasional storm and regain his equilibrium more readily than if self-esteem is low. He will be more able to make informed decisions. He will usually be more willing to try new ways of doing things, learning from mistakes and building confidence for future challenges. He will be able to recognize and develop his specific strengths and cope with changes successfully. He is more likely to enjoy life and form more successful, fulfilling relationships than someone who suffers from acute feelings of lack of self-worth, and he will tend to attract genuine liking and respect from others.

The foundations for healthy self-esteem

My observations and clinical experience indicate that there are (at the very least) seven main elements that form the foundation for social and emotional health and which thereby lead to healthy self-esteem. I believe that the interaction is reciprocal – healthy levels of self-esteem will enable the consolidation and growth of these elements. I also see them as closely inter-dependent. I have not, therefore, presented them in any hierarchical or developmental order. Although some areas may be more central to each person's feelings of self-worth than others, I believe that it is important to explore all seven areas in order to help someone to establish and maintain healthy self-esteem.

Self-knowledge

- Developing a sense of security in terms of a strong sense of self: an understanding of who 'I' am and where I fit into the social world around me.

- Developing and maintaining my personal values – my guiding principles in life.

- Understanding differences and commonalities – how I am different from others in looks and character and how I can also have things in common with others. How I can act in different ways according to the situation that I'm in.

Self and others

- Knowing how relationships function, in particular being able to develop and maintain my own identity as a separate person while still recognizing the natural *inter*dependence of relationships.

- Understanding the difficulties inherent in relationships and in learning to co-operate with each other.

- Seeing things from another person's perspective and developing an understanding of how they might see me. Learning respect and tolerance for other people's views.

- Understanding my emotions and being aware of the ways in which I express them.

- Knowing that I can choose *how* to express emotions appropriately, rather than deny or repress them or act in an inappropriate way.

- Recognizing other people's emotions and being able to distinguish my feelings from those of others.

Self-acceptance

- Knowing my own strengths and recognizing areas that I find difficult and may want to work on.

- Accepting that it is natural to make mistakes and that this is often how we learn best.

- Knowing that I am doing the best that I can with the knowledge and skills currently available to me.

- Feeling OK about my physical body.

Self-reliance

- Knowing how to take care of myself.

- Understanding that life is often difficult but there are lots of things that I can do for myself to help smooth the path.

- Building a measure of independence and self-motivation.

- Being able to self-monitor and adjust my actions, feelings and thoughts according to realistic assessments of my progress.

- Believing that I have mastery over my life and can meet challenges as and when they arise.

Self-expression

- Understanding how we communicate with each other, not just with words but also through facial expression, body posture, intonation, the clothes we wear, etc.

- Learning to 'read the signals' beyond the words so that I can understand others more successfully and also express myself more fully and congruently.

- Developing creativity in self-expression. Recognizing and celebrating the unique ways in which we each express who we are.

Self-confidence

- Knowing that my opinions, thoughts and actions have value and that I have the right to express them.

- Knowing that I have the right to be me and that I make a difference.

- Developing a creative approach to solving problems and being confident enough in my own abilities to be able to experiment with different methods of problem-solving and to be flexible enough to alter strategies if needed.

- Being able to accept challenges and to make choices.

- Being secure enough in myself to be able to develop strategies for coping successfully with the unexpected.

Self-awareness

- Developing the ability to be focused in the here and now, rather than absorbed in negative thoughts about the past or future. This includes an awareness of my feelings as they arise.

- Knowing what I am capable of, and learning to set realistic yet challenging goals.

- Understanding that emotional, mental and physical change is a natural part of my life.

- Understanding that I have some control in *how* I change and develop.

The information and activity sheets in Part III of this book are designed to enable participants to explore all seven of these elements.

Suggestions for further reading

Maslow, A.H. (1962) *Toward a Psychology of Being.* Princeton, NJ: Van Nostrand.

Rayner, E. (1993) *Human Development: An Introduction to the Psychodynamics of Growth, Maturity and Ageing.* London: Routledge.

Satir, V. (1991) *Peoplemaking.* London: Souvenir Press.

Storr, A. (1989) *Solitude.* London: Fontana.

Chapter 2

Self-Esteem and the Process of Change

A framework for change

The prospect of change can be particularly daunting for someone who has low self-esteem. Even though a person may feel anxious or distressed and may want to make changes in order to feel more at ease with himself and more at ease with others, he may feel at a loss as to how to structure these changes. Having some sort of framework can help to provide a sense of direction and to give an overview of what is happening as the process unfolds. Personal construct theory offers one such framework.

In the 1950s American psychologist George Kelly outlined a theory of personal development which we can use to look at how we make sense of our world and how we deal with change as individuals (Kelly 1955). Kelly suggested that each of us is a 'scientist' – a seeker of patterns and a hypothesis tester. He said that we test out our hypotheses (what we believe about ourselves and the world) by making experiments throughout life. Sometimes these experiments validate our hypotheses and so strengthen our belief system. Sometimes our experiments don't turn out the way we expected, so we either alter our beliefs or alter our experiment. By doing this we have the potential to be constantly 'reinventing' ourselves.

As we continue to make our experiments we find patterns in how the world operates and in how we operate within the world. Because we can see certain similarities and contrasts in what is happening in our environment, we begin to anticipate events, to predict outcomes. Kelly called the basis of these anticipations 'constructs'. For example, I may have a construct day/night. I know from experience that one follows the other and that they have different characteristics such as light/dark. I can therefore predict or anticipate that this will always be the case. All constructs have an opposite: we can't know what 'day' is if we don't have 'night' to contrast it with.

Constructs are linked together to form a hierarchical structure, and in this way the use of one construct (because it is part of a system) implies the relevance of several others. To take the example of day and night again, one association I might have with day is 'work', and for night I might also have a construct of 'sleep'. Of course, for other people this might be reversed or night could subsume the construct 'restless', and so on.

It follows that a person's constructs about themselves and about the world around them will have a profound effect on how they behave and relate to others.

The context in which constructs are used is vital and we can never assume that we know exactly what other people mean by a certain construct unless we explore it with them in more depth. One way of doing this is to find out what their opposite is for a given construct. Let's say that Person A considers herself to be 'shy', and her opposite of this is 'outgoing'. She wants to become more outgoing and explores what it would be like to change in this direction by elaborating her construct of outgoing to see what that would involve. Person B also considers herself to be shy. Her opposite of 'shy' is 'conceited'. She has no wish to make changes in this direction and sees 'shy' as a predominantly positive characteristic. However, she feels that this construct does imply some others that are not so agreeable to her.

Exploring or 'elaborating' the opposite pole can help to show the way forward. Also, trying to stop doing one thing without first elaborating an alternative doesn't usually work very successfully. Imagine saying to yourself 'Don't get anxious!' The image that you will have in your mind will be of yourself being in an anxious state, and this is very likely to trigger the actual feelings of anxiety. If you are able to elaborate the opposite of anxious and you can imagine this vividly enough, you will have a better sense of what that more desirable state entails. In this case, knowing what you are aiming for helps you to stop doing what you don't want! (See Chapter 3, 'Working with Imagery'.)

Kelly said that a person's construct system provides both freedom and constraint: the system is ever-changing, but at any one time we are limited to making choices within the structure we have invented for ourselves. We do not need to be the victim of our past, however, as there are always other pathways along which we can move so as to see ourselves in a new light.

So, according to this theory of development, when we look at what we would like to change in our lives we also need to look at some of the other constructs we have that might be affected by this change or that might be preventing us from changing. We then need to explore or elaborate the opposite side of the construct. If I want to be more outgoing, what exactly does outgoing consist of?

What makes change difficult?

Familiarity

Any change in our beliefs, thoughts or behaviours automatically entails having to give something up. As well as the positive intention to change therefore, there will often also be uncertainty and possibly some resistance. This resistance centres on letting go of what is most familiar to us. This can prove difficult. Even though what we know best may no longer be useful or could possibly be detrimental to our physical, emotional, mental or spiritual well-being, we can at least continue to predict outcomes if we stay with an old belief or behaviour.

Threat

Kelly defined threat as the awareness of an imminent change in our central or 'core' constructs. Our core constructs are the most resistant to change because they define the essence of how we see ourselves, the most important aspects of how we make sense of the world. We don't want this change to happen, so we may try to avoid or sabotage the change. Threat is extremely uncomfortable. A person who feels under threat in this way may experience the sensations associated with panic or anger.

Fear

This is described as an awareness of an imminent but smaller change. It is not as strong a feeling as threat but can still be fairly unpleasant!

Anxiety

Kelly described anxiety as the awareness that the events with which we are confronted lie outside the 'range of convenience' of our construct system. In other words, the event has not been part of our previous experience, so we can't accurately predict what is going to happen. We basically don't know what to do. Anxiety is fed by avoidance. If we don't experiment with our beliefs and behaviours, we will continue to keep our world small and manageable, avoiding changes and becoming more and more anxious. The more we avoid, the more anxious we become, because we have no experience from which we can predict possible outcomes.

Kelly argued that the way to overcome these feelings is actively to 'experiment' so that we can increase the range of our experiences.

Guilt

Another obstacle to change is the feeling of guilt. Kelly described guilt feelings as arising when we feel we are about to step, or have already stepped, outside the 'core' role structure that we have invented for ourselves. For example, if my core role is mother and this role subsumes constructs such as caring, available and loving, I am likely to feel guilt if I then step out of this role for the first time in order to go back to work and I see my caring and loving constructs as being compromised by my 'availability'. This will be especially true if some of my 'work' constructs are in direct opposition to those of 'mother'.

Guilt feelings can be very destructive. They go with the language of "I should, I ought, I must" and may lead once again to avoidance of change. In order to overcome guilt we may need to 'reframe' the change, look at it from other aspects, elaborate our new role or reach a compromise in order to make the change more manageable for ourselves.

These feelings are not mutually exclusive and can be experienced to different degrees. They provide a useful indicator of why change can sometimes be difficult. Recognition of these feelings can also provide us with a positive tool for moving on; there are always other options open to us, other experiments that we can make.

Having attended a course on personal construct theory as part of my professional training, I felt that I had a better understanding of some of my own difficulties in making the changes that I wanted in life. When I later trained as an imagework practitioner, I knew that I finally had the tools for change that suited my way of learning. Both personal construct theory and imagework look beyond *what* we think to *how* we think and what we *experience*.

Imagework contains many of the elements of personal construct theory and offers a creative way of using our natural imaginative abilities to enhance our well-being and to cope with life's challenges. Imagery now plays a large part in both my working and personal life and has become 'second nature' to me. I think this is largely due to the fact that it was always 'first nature' but I lost sight of it somewhere in my teens! The next chapter is therefore devoted to the exploration of imagery and imagework.

Suggestions for further reading

Dalton, P. and Dunnett, G. (1990) *A Psychology for Living: Personal Construct Theory for Professionals and Clients.* Self-published: Dunton Publishing.

Fransella, F. and Dalton, P. (1990) *Personal Construct Counselling in Action.* London: Sage.

Kelly, G.A. (1955) *The Psychology of Personal Constructs.* New York: Norton.

Chapter 3

Working with Imagery

What are images?

We are all able to 'think' in images. In fact, images are constantly being transmitted from our unconscious to our conscious minds. These images are a natural part of our lives and are our earliest means of making sense of the world. They form the basis of our knowledge about ourselves and others and about our environment before we are ever able to communicate through words. They also therefore form the basis for how we anticipate events (see Chapter 2).

When we are using our conscious mind, we are most actively engaged with the outside world. The conscious mind is generally goal-oriented and productive. It likes order and responds well to structured activities but it doesn't cope particularly well with change (Markova 1996).

'Below-the-surface' thinking is the province of the unconscious mind. This level is where we 'store' our experiences and, perhaps more importantly, our perceptions of the world in the form of images of one sort or another. Throughout life we are constantly building up a memory bank of these internal images.

> Deeply held symbols, of which we are not necessarily aware, structure our thoughts, feelings, attitudes and actions. It is perfectly possible to operate all our lives without ever investigating these internal images or programs, but then we will have very little choice about who we are and where we are going. (Glouberman 1992, p.2)

Take a few moments now to imagine that you are sitting in your garden or in a park on a warm, sunny day. In your imagination become aware of your surroundings. What can you see?... What can you hear?... What can you feel?... What can you smell?... You may be able to see yourself in the garden or park as though you are watching a film... Or perhaps you experience it as though you are in the film... You may have a 'sense' of an image but not a clear picture... Perhaps your image is more heavily based on sounds or smells...or on feelings...or perhaps a combination of these...

This is an important point to remember – when we talk of images we are not just referring to something that can be visualized. Some people can 'see' things clearly in their imagination, others may get a sense of an image but not a clear picture. Some people have mostly auditory or feeling images; others have mostly kinaesthetic (sensation) images.

There is no right or wrong way of perceiving an image, and even if two people have the same image they will *experience* it very differently. Each person's imagery is unique to him or her. It represents their own personal way of relating to themselves and the world, their own personal way of thinking.

Have you ever been so 'lost in thought' that you were unaware of what was going on around you? Have you ever solved a problem or remembered someone's name when you were supposedly doing something completely unrelated? Do you ever catch yourself singing a tune in your head that you're sure you haven't heard recently? Or have you ever felt a strong emotion and wondered 'Where on earth did *that* come from?' These are some of the times when you have tapped into your unconscious, and through the power of images your unconscious mind has had a direct effect on your conscious world.

By thinking about yourself in a garden or park you were also bringing stored images into your imagination, but this time through choice. The imagination acts like a 'meeting place' between your conscious and your unconscious mind, a 'common ground where both meet on equal terms and create a life experience that combines the elements of both' (Johnson 1989, p.140).

The imagination also connects the mind, body and emotions. The mind and body are in constant communication with each other, as different systems of the body respond to messages from the mind and vice versa. Images play an important role in this communication. For example, the imagination directly affects the autonomic nervous system (ANS) – that part of our nervous system that controls such things as heart rate, breathing, circulation, body temperature and digestive processes. The ANS basically helps us to maintain the constancy of our internal environment. The system has two parts – the sympathetic and the parasympathetic. The parasympathetic division of the ANS conserves body resources. The sympathetic division increases body activity and utilizes resources. How can images affect such a complex system? If I tell myself to increase my heart rate or sweat, I'm not likely to notice much response! But if I imagine a frightening event or am anticipating a difficult situation like giving a presentation, then my body will respond accordingly.

> …imagery does seem to have a set of unique qualities which include a powerful ability to connect us with parts of us that words do not reach – in particular, thoughts, feelings, intuitions, and body functions that are normally unconscious. (Glouberman 1992, pp.21–22)

In fact, our imaginings can have such a powerful effect on our bodies that we can experience an event as though it were actually happening – or perhaps even more intensely than it would be in reality. For many people, memories and expectations are so strong that the past and future are not *as* real but *more* real than the present.

Of course, the unconscious is much more than just a depository of the past. Austrian psychoanalyst Carl Jung described the unconscious as 'a living psychic entity which, it seems, is relatively autonomous, behaving as if it were a personality with intentions of its own' (Jung 1990, p.17).

> Completely new thoughts and creative ideas can present themselves from the unconscious – thoughts that have never been conscious before. They grow up from the dark depths of the mind like a lotus and form a most important part of the subliminal psyche. (Jung 1978, p.25)

The richness and creativity of our unconscious mind and the abundance of images available to us means that we have the opportunity to understand ourselves more fully and make more informed choices in life. It is also possible to create new images that will work for us. These can replace or outweigh old stored images, formed through past experience, that are no longer useful for our self-development. Such creativity allows for the possibility of challenging old belief systems and of creating a positive future for ourselves.

For much of the time, however, our minds are so full of thoughts and preoccupations that there is very little space left for these symbols and creative ideas to come to the surface! We therefore need to 'invite' images into our imagination if we want to work with them in a constructive way.

Imagework is a tool with which to create some of that much-needed space and facilitate the exploration of the images that can then expand into our more conscious awareness.

What is imagework?

The term 'imagework' is used by psychotherapist and trainer, Dr Dina Glouberman, to describe a particular way of working with images. She refers to this work as 'in its broadest sense, a method of tapping into, exploring, and changing the images that guide our lives'.

> Imagework is basically a training in using images more effectively to understand and change our lives. It includes developing the receptive ability to tune into the images that guide us, and the active ability to create new images that enhance our health, happiness, and creativity. (Glouberman 1992, p.6)

Imagework is applicable to all areas of life and is not a specific 'therapy'.

The idea of working with personal images is not new, of course. The process is centuries old and played an important part in the healing traditions of many ancient cultures. In the 19th century, Carl Jung encouraged his patients to use 'active imagination' as a self-help tool. The process of active imagination is similar to dreaming, except that you are fully awake and conscious during the experience. In active imagination the events take place on the imaginative level, where the person 'invites' an image to emerge from the unconscious and then actively involves herself in that image. Use of active imagination starts from the premise that the unconscious has its own wisdom, so although the person is participating fully in the process, she allows her imagination to flow where it wants and then works with whatever images arise. Robert Johnson describes how by talking to your images and interacting with them in this way you invariably find that 'they tell you things you never consciously knew and express thoughts that you never consciously thought' (Johnson 1989, p.138).

Imagework takes the process into new realms by allowing us to explore our present reality from the *perspective* of our images – to experience the image by 'stepping in to it' or 'becoming it'.

> The images that come in this way have a powerful ability to sum up with a telling metaphor the basic structure of whatever it is you are asking about. The metaphor tends to be so accurate that the more you explore it, the more it can be seen to correspond on every level and in every detail not only with the specific problem but even with your life as a whole. The implicit suddenly becomes explicit, the complexities of the problem become streamlined into a simple structure, the history of the situation becomes obvious, and suddenly a resolution emerges where it seemed impossible before. (Glouberman 1992, p.89)

We should not assume that an image can be directly translated into a given meaning (rather like an 'image dictionary'). Each image is intimately connected with an individual's personal and cultural history and will be influenced by where, when and how it was created. James Hillman refers to this process as 'an imagination service, not an information service' (Moore 1990). He suggests that we do not need to interpret the images that arise but that the image itself is more important, more inclusive and more complex than what we have to say about it. We need the image itself, not the explanation, to help us on our path.

In other words, images demand respect not analysis! It is important to remember this when helping others to use their imagination. We can encourage them to talk about their images and to talk with their images but should resist any temptation to offer our own interpretations as to what they might mean.

However, once an image, or set of images, has been worked with for a while it is often possible for the 'image-maker' to make a tentative 'mapping' on to actual life. The individual may experience an 'aha' sensation ("that feels right") which leads to a shift in perception and opens up possibilities for movement and change where none seemed evident before.

> Once we have entertained an image, it is always potentially present to our gaze… This is the basis of art therapy or journal keeping: making a home for certain images that have been transforming. (Moore 1996, pp.64–65)

Imagework allows the integration of left-brain logical thinking with the right-brain holistic overview in order to reach creative solutions to life's challenges. It is homeopathic rather than allopathic. It helps you to befriend a problem rather than make an enemy of it, and in this sense it is basically a solution-focused, rather than a problem-focused, approach.

Imagework also gives us the opportunity to:

- observe ourselves doing something
- make connections between cause and effect
- see how a 'key' moment is the spur to something else happening
- do it and learn *how* to do it at the same time
- experiment with different outcomes
- work through difficult feelings
- explore different perspectives
- experiment with setting goals.

Summary

Because of the perpetual interaction between the mind and the body, if I believe something about myself strongly enough I am likely to experience it in my life in actuality. For example, if I believe that I am 'shy' or 'clumsy' then I will have a picture of myself in different situations acting in a 'shy' or 'clumsy' way. I will not be projecting a positive image of myself onto future events and I will act in the way that I imagined, so continuing to reaffirm this picture of myself. In other words, telling myself how badly I am going to do in some activity may in fact lead to actual poor performance – my imagination results in a self-fulfilling prophecy.

My belief is that a person with perpetual low self-esteem has what might be referred to as 'negative image patterning'. For example, an image that a person might have of herself failing in one situation inter-connects with a myriad other images so that she eventually sees herself as 'a person who fails'.

Providing a person with the means to foster creative use of the imagination can help them to build a unified sense of their inner and outer worlds; can enable them to see events, problems, and challenges from a different viewpoint; and can help them to find the way forward that is most appropriate for their individual needs. The resultant ability to make better-informed choices in life will surely lead to a feeling of control, more-effective learning and more-fulfilling relationships. In fact, the imagination is a natural resource that none of us can afford to ignore!

Suggestions for further reading

Glouberman, D. (2003) *Life Choices, Life Changes: Develop Your Personal Vision with Imagework.* London: Hodder and Stoughton.

Johnson, R.A. (1989) *Inner Work: Using Dreams and Active Imagination for Personal Growth.* New York: HarperSanFrancisco.

Jung, C.G. (ed) (1978) *Man and His Symbols.* London: Pan Books (Picador edition).

Plummer, D. (2001) *Helping Children to Build Self-Esteem.* London: Jessica Kingsley Publishers.

Chapter 4

Transfer and Maintenance of Skills

From the very beginning of a course of this nature, facilitators need to keep in mind strategies for promoting self-help skills. Progress towards increased self-motivation and maintenance of healthy self-esteem can only be achieved when a person has had ample experience of identifying his own needs and working out his own solutions to his difficulties. As facilitators, we can offer the space, time and possible strategies for this learning to take place, but it is crucial to build in more and more 'do at home' activities and chances for group members to facilitate each other from as early as possible in the course.

Supporting someone in building his self-esteem must inevitably involve some assumptions on our part. If we make these assumptions transparent to him, we can encourage the 'go it alone' element in a variety of ways.

Most obviously, we can make it clear that we believe that everyone is capable of facilitating their own learning and development. We must be prepared, therefore, to give accurate, descriptive feedback to individuals as they make changes themselves and also when they are involved in facilitating others. We need to ensure that, in a group situation, individuals are aware of how to give positive feedback to each other and that we, in turn, remember to comment positively on the quality of the feedback! As each person begins to recognize their skills and abilities, we need to withdraw gradually from this role and encourage realistic self-evaluations.

Another useful assumption to make is that each person will *already* be doing something, however small, that is moving them towards their preferred future. Again our task as facilitator is to help individuals to identify what it is that they are already doing that is helping them to achieve their goals.

Carl Rogers formulated certain hypotheses about the learning process which are useful to bear in mind with regard to the maintenance of progress in the context of a self-esteem group (Rogers 1969):

Significant learning is more likely to take place when the subject matter is seen as being of relevance to the student. It is important to encourage individuals constantly to ask themselves the question 'How is this relevant to me?' as they work through the various activities and information sheets (see information sheet 1B, p.116).

Learning that involves a change in self-perception may be threatening and can be resisted. We need to talk about this as being a natural part of the change process for some people and offer practical strategies for moving through resistances when the person is ready to do so. See Chapter 2 'Self-Esteem and the Process of Change' and also the Section 5 activity and information sheets 'The Challenge of Change' (p.150–166).

Learning that could inlvolve a threat to the self is more easily abosrbed when external pressures are at a minimum. Our role here is to ensure as far as possible that the group is a supporting, understanding environment in which change can take place. It is also important to encourage individuals to make use of existing support networks outside the group and to be active in establishing contact with people who will continue to be supportive of the changes they are making (see information sheet 1B, p.116).

Important learning often takes place through doing. Discussion and reading really are not enough! Experiencing the imagework within the group and being able (and willing) to apply the activities outside the group are absolutely vital to an individual's success in making changes. It is important to keep referring to this as you work through the sessions together. Participants need to identify how, when and where they can use what they are learning.

Learning is enhanced when students take a responsible part in the learning process. It may be that some course participants had experience of a very different way of learning in the past. They may have memories of 'being taught' a subject with little or no active participation on their part. A more interactive group may be particularly difficult for them to adjust to. It can also be quite painful for some people to be reflective and proactive in their learning. It requires taking responsibility for oneself, which can feel very frightening, particularly if you have low self-esteem. The 'check-in' groups (see p.48) can help in this process, and I strongly recommend that they be incorporated from the very start of the course.

Learning that involves feelings as well as interest is usually the most lasting and comprehensive. We all know that when something suddenly 'grabs our interest' and 'fires our enthusiasm' we are usually much more willing to spend time and energy exploring it. We also know that experiences that help us to change the way we feel about ourselves and the world can leave a lasting impression. Imagework is particularly effective in helping people to connect thoughts, feelings and actions in a safe way.

Independence, creativity and self-reliance are supported when self-evaluation is primary, and evaluation by others is secondary. The whole structure of a self-esteem course should revolve around this principle. As mentioned before, we are aiming to encourage realistic self-evaluation through the activities undertaken and through our facilitation – giving accurate 'commentary' on what individuals are doing and then gradually lessening this commentary and encouraging individuals to take over that task for themselves.

Most socially useful learning involves understanding the learning process and being open to experience. If participants understand the reasons for doing each of the activities and have an understanding of the overall processes, they are much more likely to be able to generalize their learning into everyday situations. Imagework is a hugely adaptable tool. Once an individual understands the principles, they will be able to modify imagework exercises for their own needs. It does no harm to labour this point! Imagework is not a set of 'follow the instruction' exercises and 'always do it this way for evermore'! The structure provided by having a general theme throughout the sessions, together with repeated patterns of imagery, will help participants to establish a familiar format for problem-solving and goal-setting, which they can then be guided to use in a variety of situations. In this way, individuals can be encouraged in the development of their imaginative and creative skills to support the changes they are making in all areas of their lives.

In summary, a person is most likely to be able to maintain progress if she:

- is aware of what she is already doing to reach her desired future

- believes that what she is aiming for is personally relevant, achievable and beneficial to herself

- knows from the start what might make things difficult

- has support and encouragement from others

- sets her own realistic yet challenging goals and takes one small step at a time

- takes an active part in finding her own solutions to difficulties

- takes time to recognize and reap the benefits of the goals she has already achieved (enjoys the process!)

- is able to reflect on her successes and failures and realistically self-evaluate (i.e. does not always rely on others to evaluate her progress)

- recognizes 'failures' as being a form of feedback – an indication of how to modify her actions or thoughts

- understands the processes and steps that have led to each success and is able to generalize these to other situations.

Suggestion for further reading

Rogers, C. (1969) *Freedom to Learn: A View of What Education Might Become.* Columbus, OH: Merrill. (See Chapters 7 and 8.)

Chapter 5

Working with Groups

Why work on self-esteem in a group setting? There are many advantages to this approach. Groups offer the opportunity for:

- 'on the spot' peer support which could be extended beyond the life of the group

- pooling resources and ideas

- learning and building on social skills

- reducing the facilitator's 'teacher'/'magician' status

- encouraging self-help

- active experimentation to try out new ways of 'being'

- active engagement in the learning process

- spontaneity and creativity as participants try out ideas with more than one person

- encouraging tolerance and respect of other people's ideas

- experience of positive interaction with peers.

The disadvantages are mainly in respect of the time and energy needed by group facilitators:

- Groups take a lot of organizing in the early stages. You will need a variety of activities and materials to allow for a variety of learning styles.

- You need to be aware of how groups function and that you will be encouraging 'group-esteem' as well as individual self-esteem.

- It may take some members a long time to 'find their feet' in a group.

- It may be more tempting to give advice or take over the group during group discussions than if you were working with someone one-to-one.

- This may be the only social contact that some group members experience and they may unwittingly sabotage their own progress in order to have continued support from the group.

Organizing a group

There are a few issues that need to be addressed with any group. Whatever you decide about these, you need to be clear about the reasons for your decisions and be ready to evaluate the group and review your policies for the next time around. I have, through circumstances rather than informed choice, been faced with all sorts of combinations of group participants. Sometimes, combinations that I originally thought might not work well (e.g. because of differences in age or, in one case, having only one woman in a group with six men) have made for a very cohesive and supportive group because of the personalities of the people involved. Having said this, in general it is best not to have one member who, due to age difference, for example, is in danger of feeling isolated because they feel they have little in common with the rest of the group. These then are the main questions you might want to consider:

- Should ages be matched?

- Should the group be single or mixed sex?

- How many is a good number? (I usually work with groups of 6 to 8.)

- Should the group be closed or open to newcomers once it has started?

Structuring the environment

It is extremely important for self-esteem groups to have structure and continuity. Roles and boundaries need to be clearly set out right at the beginning of the group. This may seem obvious and is important for most types of group work. However, in the context of self-esteem, the facilitator is responsible for demonstrating and encouraging the respect and acceptance that the group members may be lacking elsewhere in their lives (externally and/or internally). Virginia Satir writes:

> Feelings of worth can only flourish in an atmosphere where individual differences are appreciated, mistakes are tolerated, communication is open, and rules are flexible – the kind of atmosphere that is found in a nurturing family. (Satir 1991, p.26)

Environments that are most effective in enhancing self-esteem are those in which group members:

- perceive a sense of warmth and acceptance
- are offered a degree of security that allows them to grow and to try out new things without an overriding concern about failure
- are respected as individuals
- have their ideas and initiatives encouraged
- are invited to express opinions
- recognize that there are clear and definite limits within the environment
- know that rules and standards are reasonable and allow for alteration as situations change
- have a chance to succeed at their own levels.

The physical environment

Facilities

Make sure that the room you are using does not provide through access for others during a session. Do think about tea, coffee and soft drinks facilities, and establish at the beginning of the course how this will be funded and who will share responsibility for making sure that supplies are kept topped up.

Layout

It is important to have a relaxed informal setting for groups. One way to promote this is for the facilitator to set up a circle of comfortable chairs before group members arrive. Remove extra chairs when you know for sure that someone isn't coming to the session but don't remove chairs if you think someone is just going to be late. It is very difficult to join a group session that has already started and doubly difficult if you have low self-esteem. It is also obviously very disruptive to have to ask the whole group to shuffle round in order to fit in an extra chair. Tell the group right at the beginning that the empty chair is for X, who you believe will be joining the group a little later this time. Be overt in welcoming that person into the circle when they arrive. When you feel it is appropriate, encourage them to contribute something so that they hear their own voice and are acknowledged by the others. A circle enables everyone to keep eye contact when appropriate and allows individual members of the group to take part more easily.

Breaks

If you are going to have a scheduled break make it very clear how long you are suggesting for this during the first session. This can become a real bone of contention amongst group members if some are keen to restart on time and others amble back ten minutes later. However, it may be that group members need the chance to talk informally during a slightly longer break than you had originally planned. If an activity has been particularly challenging just before a break, participants may need extra time to relax afterwards. Late returners may be indicating something about how they are feeling! You might want to involve the group in negotiating timings after the first session. This will also introduce the idea of participants having more say in how the group evolves. Breaks are not just 'added extras', they can in fact be a very valuable part of the session.

Ensuring physically comfortable and pleasant surroundings for meetings is a sign of how much value we place on the group, how much we respect the group members and how much we respect ourselves as facilitators. This may mean arriving at the venue early enough to switch the heating on and arrange the room before anyone else arrives. It may mean allowing yourself enough time to have a few quiet moments of reflection on your own before the session starts.

Facilitating groups

The role of facilitator

I strongly recommend that all groups should have two facilitators. It is very difficult to 'hold' a group and to be aware of everything that is going on within and between all the group members. Having two facilitators gives you the chance to share ideas, keep better track of what is happening and share the responsibility for planning, carrying out and evaluating the sessions. It is also important for each facilitator to be able to reflect on their skills as a group leader and to be able to debrief at the end of each session. This is much harder if you are only able to do this infrequently with a peer or at a scheduled supervision session.

As facilitator, you have responsibility for setting the initial mood or atmosphere of the group experience. However much you may intend for this to be a collaborative group, the initial sessions will undoubtedly involve a greater degree of input from you than later on in the course. This needs to be handled sensitively to discourage or pre-empt any teacher/student expectations that group members may have. The following are some general principles for facilitating groups (see also suggestions for further reading at the end of this chapter):

- Help individuals to clarify their own reasons for being in the group. Be aware that there may be conflicting aims or misunderstandings about the purpose of the group, which will need to be addressed from the outset. Have clear objectives in mind for each session.

- Help the group to establish guidelines for the 'life' of the group and offer periodic reminders if necessary (see 'Establishing group guidelines', p.47).

- Help the group to stay on track when they are working in pairs and in larger group work but avoid being prescriptive.

- Aim to promote communication between group members as often as possible. Participants should be encouraged to direct their questions and comments directly to each other with the facilitator keeping things moving.

- Do not underestimate or devalue your own abilities. Offer your knowledge as a 'resource' for the group. Occasional self-disclosure of feelings and thoughts can be helpful but should not be too frequent. Be honest about what you do and don't know. A self-evaluation sheet is included at the end of the chapter. I recommend that you fill in at least one of these for each session and discuss it with your co-facilitator or supervisor.

- Introduce only a limited amount of new material each session. Encourage personal contributions from participants about their own experiences of using the strategies that have been discussed and tried out in the sessions. Use a stepped approach to learning, building on previous sessions.

- Aim to use a variety of materials/approaches to support different learning styles. You may find it helpful to use a planning sheet such as the one included at the end of this chapter. Be aware that some people like to get an overview of what they are working towards first. They can then 'slot in' the smaller chunks of information. Others like to collect smaller pieces of information first and then fit these into their own 'bigger picture'. Some people find written information sheets useful, others prefer to listen and absorb, yet others will learn best by 'doing' but may want information sheets to back up their learning.

- Discourage lengthy problem-focused discussions and re-telling of 'how things went wrong'. Acknowledge the difficulties experienced and steer the group towards a solution-focused approach.

- Allow participants to 'discover' things for themselves. If you feel tempted to give advice, use this as a cue to yourself first to ask the person what they feel they could do and second to ask the group for ideas. Respect the individual's ability to make choices, even if these differ from those you might like to suggest.

- Be aware that 'cosy', amenable groups are not always the ones that make the most progress. Encourage creative debates!

- Look for opportunities to allow more reticent members to speak.

- Be sensitive but firm with participants who tend to dominate the group.

- Be willing for some problems to be unresolved. It is not your role to try and make everything better!

- If someone comes up with something important right at the end of a session, do acknowledge the importance but be clear that you are not able to discuss it at that point. For example: 'This is a big issue and it deserves a lot of time, not just the few minutes we can give it now. Let's be sure to talk about it next time.' You might also check out with the person if there is someone else they can talk it over with before the next meeting.

- Be enthusiastic!

Taking care of yourself

When working with others it's important to remember that we will be most effective if we maintain and build on our own sense of self-worth and competency. If a person feels OK about herself she is much more likely to be supportive, accepting and nurturing of others. This in turn will help the other person to grow in confidence and to develop and maintain effective strategies for coping with life's difficulties. In the words of Carl Rogers, the other person will become 'more unique and more self-expressive' and 'more similar to the person he would like to be' (Rogers 1961, p.38). With this in mind, here are a few key points for you to think about:

- Listen to your body. Recognize your own feelings and take responsibility for them.

- Keep a note of what worked well in each session and what needs to be changed or adapted.

- Make use of your co-facilitator for debriefing after sessions.

- Take care of yourself physically. Give yourself adequate time before and after the group to do whatever you need to do in order to feel relaxed and confident.

- Have fun! Enjoy the group and the processes that you are exploring together.

Establishing group guidelines

It is always useful to establish a set of group 'guidelines' and to remind the group of these periodically, if needed. Such guidelines might include the following:

- Respect other people and their contributions to the group. Avoid judging or criticizing.

- The group will start and finish on time.

- No alcohol/drugs to be brought into the group.

- Anything said within the group is confidential and cannot be shared with non-group members unless there are issues of safety involved. (See also activity sheet 1.4, 'Communication guidelines', p.114.)

Warm-ups

New groups require time spent in getting to know each other. It is important to build up your own repertoire of group 'warm-up' activities to help participants to feel relaxed about sharing their thoughts and ideas. I have a personal aversion to 'gelling' games for adults – I have had to endure them in too many groups that I have attended as a participant! My personal preference is for simpler 'getting to know you' activities in pairs and threes to start with. I have, however, included two slightly more active questionnaire exercises in the activity sheets in recognition of the fact that not everyone will feel like me about such activities.

Using appropriate role models and peer facilitators

People often learn best from others who have been through similar circumstances and have 'come through'. Time and again, when asked to identify the single most useful aspect of working in a group, clients have reported the benefit of being with others 'just like me'. They have also referred to the usefulness of hearing how others have dealt successfully with difficult situations and have made progress throughout the life of the group. In many instances, clients have reported being motivated by the successes of others and by the support that individual group members can offer to each other in the setting of goals and the realistic monitoring of successes and difficulties.

Group facilitators should seriously consider the possibility of inviting previous group members to come and talk to new groups, but this needs to be timely in order for the group to feel motivated and supported in their own struggles. Too early, and it could lead to demotivation; too late, and the impact will be lessened.

The life of a group – the beginning phase

Groups hold all sorts of different associations for people; this aspect needs to be recognized and explored as early as possible. Coming to a group may initially heighten feelings of inadequacy, being different, depending on others (I can't cope on my own), and so on. Perhaps some participants arrive wanting, or even demanding, a 'quick cure' and feeling disheartened when they discover that change of this nature is going to take time and commitment. Others arrive full of hope and ready to take a leap of faith into unknown territory, possibly without any safety net! A primary task in this phase of the course is therefore helping group members to get to grips with the whole idea of being in a group and of 'finding their place' (see activity sheets 1.1–1.5, pp.111–115).

Using 'check-in groups' and closing circles

During the early sessions in particular, you may find that a few people have been very verbal or have taken up a large proportion of the allocated time because they were working on a particular issue in more depth.

One way of ensuring that everyone feels 'heard' and feels part of the group is to ask everyone to check in with how they are feeling at the start and then have a closing circle where everyone says one thing before they leave.

CHECKING IN

Where there are six or more participants it is better to facilitate the 'check-in' times by splitting into smaller groups of three or four. The full format for these groups is outlined below. I have experienced the power of this in a variety of groups with mixed ages and sexes. I do, however, use an adapted form at times if I think the group would find it too difficult to sit with eyes closed or to sit silently between speakers at this early stage of the course.

Sit in a close circle and make contact of some sort (e.g. one hand on the arm of the chairs either side of you or feet just touching). Close eyes. Relax. Tune into yourself. Notice what your body is feeling. Notice where your thoughts are drifting to. Be aware of the other people in the small group, then tune back into yourself again. The first person to speak takes one minute (this can be extended as the weeks progress) to talk about how they are feeling or anything else that comes to mind at that moment. The other members of the group simply listen. The speaker is told when their one minute is coming to an end. As facilitator you could say something such as 'Start to draw that to a close now' or 'Just finishing what you are saying…'. The speaker then sits quietly for a few moments while the listeners silently 'send' their complete acceptance. The speaker is asked to be open to receive this acceptance. This may seem a difficult concept for some at first, but explain that there is no right or wrong way of doing this. Group members do not talk between speakers. After a few moments ask everyone to tune back into themselves, and then the next person in the circle has their chance to speak. Repeat the process for each person in the group. When everyone has had their turn, they can open their eyes and spend five minutes giving each other any feedback as appropriate. The feedback must of course be non-judgemental. It could be something like: 'I really felt for you when you said…'; 'I think I know how you feel when…'; 'You sounded excited when you talked about…'

So for these check-in groups to work well you need to establish the format beforehand with the group:

- Explain that they will have their eyes closed so that, as speakers, they can concentrate on what they are feeling and on what they want to say rather than thinking about any feedback they might or might not get from the others in the group. As listeners, they can focus on listening to what is being said.

- Explain that it is fine if they don't feel like talking for the whole time allotted but that their turn will still be the same length as everyone else's.

- Explain about 'sending' and 'receiving' acceptance.

- Explain the type of feedback that is acceptable for the end of the check-in period.

Throughout the course you can gradually increase the time for each person to speak when this feels right, but maximum time should be five minutes (three minutes is usually ample). Ideally you should have equal numbers in each mini circle. Keep an eye on the time and don't be tempted to give some people longer than others. After the first few times of doing this you could begin to use this time for people to check in with how they feel about a given topic. For example, everyone says whatever comes to mind on the topic of confidence or relationships or anger.

I first came across this format when I was doing my imagework training. Dina Glouberman refers to this as 'Oekos groups' from the Greek word for home. It is an amazingly effective way of ensuring that everyone has their turn and that everyone feels that they have been listened to and accepted for who they are.

CLOSING CIRCLES

At the end of each meeting bring everyone back together again in a circle and finish with each person having the chance to say one brief thing before they leave. This closing circle can be more structured than the check-in groups. I usually offer an idea for people to complete in their own words. For example:

I feel...

Today I found out that...

Today I felt...

My name is and I am...

I have noticed that...

I feel really good about…

My next step is…

I want to say that…

Today this group has given me…

My positive intention is… (see Part II, Section 2, 'Summary' (p.67)

Middles and ends

By the time the group sessions are half way through you will probably have found that people are beginning to regroup and form different bonds. They are beginning to 'find' their role in the group. Sometimes this role can be gently challenged so that people can experiment with change. For example, someone who always agrees with whatever anyone else says can be encouraged to go first in a round and to put forward their own idea before anyone else.

For some group members, ending the group will be a natural stage and will not cause any undue concerns. For others, the ending of a group may feel like a great loss, and what they experience may reflect how they deal with endings generally in life. You will need to prepare for the ending of the group well in advance. I suggest that you might start to mention it at least two weeks before the final session. Talk about what will happen next, about self-help and continuing to set goals, about saying goodbye to each other; about how they can capitalize on what they have learned. There may be some disappointments about what has not been achieved, as well as recognition of successes, and these also need to be voiced and acknowledged. Although all these things will have been discussed throughout the course, it is useful to bring all the 'threads' together in the final few weeks.

You may feel that it would be useful for groups to meet up again for a follow-up a few weeks after the course has finished. This can be very beneficial in that people have the chance to catch up on what has been happening with the others and to talk about their successes. They can perhaps support each other in problem-solving something specific that they would like to work on. However, be aware that regular follow-ups, run by the same facilitator each time, could encourage dependency rather than self-help.

Make sure that there is opportunity for a celebration in the last session. This could so easily be missed out because of lack of time or because it is not given due importance. It is, however, very important to complete the group in this way. It defines the end of the life of the group as it stands. It gives weight to acknowledging everyone's achievements and it shows that enjoyment and celebration are part of building self-esteem.

Suggestions for further reading

Dwivedi, K.N. (ed) (1999) *Group Work with Children and Adolescents: A Handbook.* London: Jessica Kingsley Publishers.

Ernst, S. and Goodison, L. (1992) *In Our Own Hands: A Book of Self-Help Therapy.* London: The Women's Press.

Houston, G. (1990) *The Red Book of Groups.* London: The Rochester Foundation.

Jacobs, M. (1992) *Swift to Hear. Facilitating Skills in Listening and Responding.* London: SPCK.

Self-evaluation of activities

Brief description of activity:

Planned duration:

Objectives:

Was the activity of an appropriate length? Was the level right for the whole group?

Did I introduce and summarize it effectively? Did I achieve my objectives?

If I were to do a similar activity again would I change it in any way? Why?
What would I do differently?

How would I extend/alter the activity to move the group on to the next stage when they are ready?

Planning Sheet for Self-Esteem Course

Date	Topic	Ideas for whole group	Ideas for smaller groups

Part II

Instructions for Self-Esteem Activities

Introduction

Using the information sheets

The information sheets may not be suitable as handouts for all groups but can be used by facilitators as a basis for discussion. I have suggested further reading for some of these sheets, but this is not essential to being able to lead the discussions.

Using the activity sheets

Most of the activity sheets are self-explanatory, and many could be used for 'do at home' exercises if you feel this is appropriate. I suggest that most groups should certainly be aiming to increase the amount that they try things outside the group as the course progresses. This, in itself, encourages an attitude of self-sufficiency and competence (see Chapter 5 'Working with Groups'). Each of the summary sheets that conclude Sections 2 to 11 links with the following section to give a logical flow to the different areas covered.

As already noted in the Introduction, the majority of the information and activity sheets can also be used in individual work with clients and pupils.

General guidelines for facilitating imagery exercises

The imagery exercises presented in Parts II and III of this book are mostly adapted from more in-depth imagework exercises formulated by Dina Glouberman (e.g. Glouberman 2003) or they have 'emerged' while I have been facilitating group sessions. A few are the result of combining exercises from both neurolinguistic programming and imagework.

Imagery exercises lend themselves to being highly interactive. As a facilitator, you will find it useful if participants give you an indication of what is happening with their images as they work with them. This will help you to pace your instructions and allows time to those who need to explore images more deeply or who are having difficulty getting an image in the first place. Verbal feedback of this kind also fosters feelings of connectedness between group members. I have suggested relevant questions that you might ask in conjunction with each imagery section.

When you are waiting for participants to produce their own images in a group, ask them to raise a finger rather than calling out to indicate that they have thought of one. This avoids disrupting others who have not yet 'found' their image.

Invariably the group will not all be working at the same pace. Move on when it feels right to do so.

Most people are able to access images in one-to-one sessions but some may find this harder in a group, especially if they feel there is a 'right' way of getting an image. You will need to assure everyone at the outset that whatever images emerge for them are OK. If someone indicates that they are having difficulty you can help them by using any or all of the following suggestions:

- There is plenty of time. As you watch just let the image come to you.

- Don't worry if the image is a bit hazy to start with. It will gradually become clearer as you work with it.

- Imagine that the nothingness that you can see is a dark curtain. As you draw the curtain aside notice what image emerges.

- If you *could* see an image, what would it be?

- Don't worry if you are having difficulty seeing the image clearly; just get a sense of what it might be and work with that.

Section 1

Getting Started

Aims of this section

- to give an overview of the course content
- to introduce the concept of self-help
- to begin to establish group identity and cohesion

Information and activity sheets

INFORMATION SHEET 1A: INTRODUCTION (P.110)

This information sheet can be given to participants prior to the start of the course and/or used as a basis for group discussion during the first session. It is important to establish the idea that the course is based on self-help and that the aim is to assist each member of the group to find their own way to build self-esteem successfully.

You will need to be familiar with the basic concepts underpinning the use of imagery and personal construct theory (see Part I, Chapters 2 and 3) in order to be able to explain these points more fully if questioned. However, this is also a good opportunity to establish the idea that opinions and suggestions are welcomed from all group members and that, once they know each other a little better, participants may want to say what they understand by each of the points on subsequent information sheets.

1.1 GETTING TO KNOW THE GROUP (P.111)

This is one way of getting people moving around and speaking to others in a relaxed way. Set a time limit (maximum of ten minutes) according to the size of the group.

An alternative way of doing this is to have a collection of cards on which there are single words or pictures of things people might like to do or like to eat. For example your list might include such things as watching soap operas, chocolate, cycling, singing, dogs, football, burgers, and so on. Try to include some that you think only one or two people might like. Distribute the cards evenly around the group. Each person has to get rid of cards by asking the question 'Do you like _____?' and handing over the appropriate card if the other person says 'Yes'. At the same time they have to find out as many names as possible. The aim is to have as few cards as you can by the end of the time limit. This does, of course, require honesty in saying if you like something or not!

1.2 REMEMBERING NAMES (P.112)

This could also be done by asking everyone to come up with a way that they would like to be described, using adjectives beginning with the first letter of their name, e.g. cool Cathy, stylish Steve, relaxed Rajeeve.

1.3 BEING PART OF A GROUP (P.113)

To be completed individually and then discussed in pairs. Ask for group contributions to the last section: 'What would help me to feel most comfortable in this group?' This could form the basis for establishing the group guidelines. Ensure that issues of confidentiality and safety are brought up at this point (see Part I, Chapter 5, 'Working with Groups').

1.4 COMMUNICATION GUIDELINES (P.114)

These also need to be incorporated into the general group 'guidelines' and revisited periodically to encourage group members to continue to use them. It is important for participants to understand the relevance of each point and the possible effects on self-esteem when these guidelines are forgotten.

Listening accurately. There are specific activities for this later in the course (activity sheet 9.5). At this stage, participants can be encouraged to listen to each other fully and try not to make assumptions about what someone else might be thinking. Talk about how a person's own anxieties may get in the way of listening accurately to someone else.

Using 'I', not 'you'. This is often a difficult task for new groups, but it is a helpful pattern to establish from the outset. Saying something like 'You know what it's like in groups, you don't want to speak up because you feel embarrassed' may well reflect what the speaker feels but is encouraging assumptions about what people feel generally in groups. If the speaker is able to say '*I* don't want to speak up because *I* feel embarrassed', this allows much greater possibility for personal change.

Another useful idea to introduce at this point is the way that we sometimes appear to hand over responsibility for how we feel to others. A statement such as 'You make me angry' assumes a very different locus of control to 'I feel angry about what you just said'.

Giving constructive feedback. This will also be revisited when the group talk about assertiveness skills (activity sheets 7.9 and 7.10). At this point group members can be encouraged to make their feedback to others positive and precise (see also guidelines for 'check-in' groups, p.49).

Recognition of personal values. This is an obvious point, but worth bringing up for discussion at the start of a group. Participants can be encouraged to reflect on the fact that they may have different guiding principles in life and, whilst we might disagree with each other over certain values, it is not the job of the group to challenge these.

Looking for the common goal. Recognizing that each person is taking part in the course because they have concerns about self-esteem (and reminding participants that this is the case) can help to clear up misunderstandings between group members. For example, on a very basic level, two people working in a pair may have different ideas about how to get something done. Keeping an eye on the fact that they both want a similar outcome may help them to come to a workable solution.

1.5 FEELINGS AND EXPECTATIONS (P.115)

To be completed individually and discussed in pairs. Common themes could be shared with the whole group to help people to recognize that they have similar worries or expectations.

INFORMATION SHEET 1B: HOW YOU CAN BENEFIT MOST FROM THIS COURSE (P.116)

Another reminder to participants that the group is a vehicle for developing self-help strategies (see Part I, Chapter 4, 'Transfer and Maintenance of Skills').

Section 2

What Is Self-Esteem?

Aims of this section

- to offer some basic information about how self-esteem develops

- to start the exploration of personal self-esteem

- to introduce the use of imagery as a way to explore personal patterns of thinking and feeling

- to introduce the idea that our thoughts have a direct effect on how we behave and develop

Information and activity sheets

INFORMATION SHEETS 2A SELF-CONCEPT AND SELF-ESTEEM AND 2B GLOBAL AND SPECIFIC SELF-ESTEEM (PP.118–119)

These information sheets can form the basis for a discussion about the fact that we can build different areas of self-esteem in our lives (instead of thinking of self-esteem only in terms of a global sense of self-worth and competency). For example, a person may feel OK about her ability and her self-worth with regard to forming friendships, but not OK about her ability to be an artist. If 'being artistic' is important in her life then any negative comments by others could potentially damage her global sense of self-esteem, unless she recognizes her abilities and self-worth in other areas.

Suggested reading

Satir, V. (1991) *Peoplemaking*. London: Souvenir Press.

Storr, A. (1989) *Solitude*. London: Fontana.

2.1 BEING SPECIFIC (P.120)

Possible areas might be:

- Relationships with friends
- Relationships with family
- Relationship with partner
- Meeting new people
- Independence
- Work
- College
- Creativity

For each broad area identified participants should then isolate one specific aspect. For example, under 'Independence' a person might identify 'travelling alone'.

2.2 FUTURE ME! (PP.121–122)

This is based on 'My future self' exercise by Dina Glouberman (2003, pp.186–191).

Each member of the group chooses a specific situation to work with. Guide the whole group through the imagery exercise. Use your own wording as this will sound more natural. The instructions on the activity sheet are there for guidance (see also 'General guidelines for facilitating imagery exercises' on p.56). Leave plenty of time between each part of the exercise for everyone to explore their chosen situation in their imagination. Ask for contributions so that the exercise feels interactive rather than static. The exchange might go something like this:

Facilitator: Imagine that it's the end of the situation now and it really didn't go well at all. Ask yourself, 'What was it that I did that meant this didn't go well?'… Would anyone like to say what went wrong?

Group member 1: I rushed and got confused.

Facilitator: OK. So rushing meant that you felt confused.

Group member 2: I didn't plan it beforehand.

Facilitator: You didn't plan it beforehand and that meant that…?

Group member 2: I felt panicky.

Facilitator: You didn't plan it beforehand so then you felt panicky… OK. So now ask yourselves, 'What was I thinking just before this situation?'

[And so on.]

2.3 EXPECTATIONS (P.123)

Draw together any links that people can come up with between thoughts and actions and the idea of self-fulfilling prophecies.

The self-fulfilling prophecy is an important concept. The idea is that whatever we expect with confidence may well happen! Our expectations have an impact on our relationships with others, and they have a powerful impact on what we become.

Our expectations come from our beliefs about ourselves and the world around us. Someone who expects things to turn out poorly and believes with absolute certainty that he will fail is obviously not setting himself up for success! A positive attitude *accompanied by realistic assessment of abilities* will invariably lead to more positive outcomes.

2.4 WHY IS IT IMPORTANT TO RAISE OUR LEVELS OF SELF-ESTEEM? (P.124)

If it has not already been discussed, this would be a good opportunity to talk about having 'healthy' levels of self-esteem rather than necessarily thinking in terms of 'high' levels of self-esteem. 'Healthy' will be wherever the individual feels comfortable with who they are. Healthy self-esteem also involves awareness of others and their needs and feelings. Building self-esteem is not about feeling so good about yourself that you lose sight of where you fit into family and friendship groups and wider society.

Brainstorm the benefits of healthy self-esteem. Possible benefits are:

- greater enjoyment of life
- increased possibility to develop specific strengths/attributes
- increased ability to deal with difficult situations
- more likely to be able to take risks
- more able to tolerate own mistakes
- better ability to cope with changes
- ability to develop secure, fulfilling relationships more easily
- ability to develop a greater understanding of other people.

See also Part I, Chapter 1, 'What Is Self-Esteem?'.

2.5 AN IMAGE OF SELF-ESTEEM (P.125)

Lead the whole group in this exercise. As before, ask for contributions every now and then. Leave plenty of pauses for people to come up with images and explore them thoroughly. The last question 'What advice do I have for "self"?' encourages people to view themselves from a different perspective. For example, my image of self-esteem at the moment of writing these words is a buttercup (I have had many different images of self-esteem over the course of writing this book, but not a buttercup before!). As the buttercup, I want to tell 'self' (Deborah) 'Chin up!' and I suddenly remember that this comes from a childhood pursuit of placing a buttercup under your chin to reflect the sunlight! (See also previous guidelines for facilitating imagery exercises, p.56.)

Take time at the end of the exercise to give everyone the chance to talk about their experience of this imagery or to show their drawing. This can be done in pairs or in the whole group.

Remind everyone that we cannot interpret images for each other. Our images have unique meanings and only the 'image-maker' will know their significance. Sometimes, talking about a personal image can help the person to clarify in their own mind what the image means to them.

2.6 PERSONAL CHECKLIST (PP.126–127)

The boxes can be shaded to the degree to which each statement is thought to be true. For example, 'Very true' would mean the whole box is shaded, 'Quite true' would mean perhaps just a small part of the box being shaded, 'Not true at all' would obviously mean no shading. This checklist could be revisited at various stages throughout the course to help participants to review their progress.

INFORMATION SHEET 2C THE ICEBERG OF SELF-ESTEEM (P.128)

Facilitate a group discussion about how little or how much we 'reveal' our emotions and thoughts. For some people, some covert aspects of a difficulty may be displayed overtly, although not necessarily in a way that might be expected. For example, embarrassment may 'appear' in the form of verbal aggression. See also information sheet 4B and activity sheet 4.2.

2.7 MY PERSONAL ICEBERG OF SELF-ESTEEM (P.129)

Brainstorm this as a whole group. Each person can then select the relevant elements for their own iceberg. This is also another tool for self-help at a later date. As some elements are reduced or eliminated there will be a knock-on effect on others so the iceberg can be redrawn. Participants can then compare the different versions of their own icebergs at different stages of the course.

The following is a compilation of sample elements from groups that I have facilitated:

Overt elements:

- fidgeting
- blushing
- looking away
- walking away
- sweating
- biting fingernails
- tearful
- tense muscles
- restricted interactions with others
- 'tongue-tied'

Covert elements:

- feeling 'awkward'
- embarrassed
- 'churned up' inside
- angry
- frustrated
- depressed
- negative self-talk
- lethargic
- 'everything is an effort'

2.8 SUMMARY (P.130)

Allocate specific time at the end of a group session for completion of the summary sheet. If it is completed within the group then there is opportunity for group members to ask questions and to seek help in formulating a positive intention if needed.

> Every experience, and every change in your experience, reflects an intention. An intention is not only a desire. It is the use of your will... If you truly desire to change [something] that change begins with the intention to change it. How it will change depends upon the intention that you set. (Zukav 1991, p.106)

Positive intentions need to be precise and stated in the first person. Even though it is an intention it should be written in the present tense as we are making an assumption that some part of it has already started to happen (see Part I, Chapter 4, 'Transfer and Maintenance of Skills'). Some examples might be:

'I am building my self-esteem'

'I am more open about how I feel in the group'

'I am expressing my opinions in group discussions'

'I am using accurate listening'

Who Am I?

Aims of this section

- to explore self-perceptions

- to extend the use of imagery as a self-help tool

- to encourage each person to recognize the important stages in his or her life journey so far

Information and activity sheets

3.1 WHO AM I? (P.132)

To be completed individually. Invite discussion about what people think makes us who we are. Are group members able to identify any unique characteristics about themselves that are not shared by any other member of the group?

3.2 CHARACTER SKETCH (P.133)

This is an adaptation of an exercise from Personal Construct Therapy (Kelly 1995). Self-characterization promotes greater awareness of self and others. It is sometimes difficult for someone with low self-esteem to conceive of how others might see them in a positive, supportive way. They may be tempted to stick to concrete things like 'She goes to X college', 'He has three children'. You may need to encourage a broader description of thoughts and feelings as well. The character sketch can be used to help the writer to identify 'themes' that might indicate particular areas of concern for them (or hidden strengths).

You could also extend this activity into thinking about how the 'character' might progress during the course of the play. If it is a three-act play spanning a two-year period how will the character be different in act three? What will they have learned? What will they be doing? How will their life have changed? What happens in act two that facilitates these changes?

Writing a second character sketch of 'future self' can help to focus a person on his goals and may also help him to identify those that are realistically achievable in the short term (see also activity sheet 2.2).

3.3 IMAGINE THAT! (PP.134–135)

Adapted from 'The image as life metaphor' exercise by Dina Glouberman (2003, pp.94–116).

Lead the whole group through this imagery exercise, following the guidelines for previous exercises (e.g. activity sheet 2.2).

Leave plenty of time (at least one hour) for discussion in pairs and in the whole group at the end. This can be a very powerful experience for some people. It is important to recognize that whatever image emerges for an individual is OK. It is simply indicating how that person is feeling about herself and her life at this particular point, and it is likely to give her some insight into how to move forward. If it has been an uncomfortable experience for anyone then it is important that she is given the chance to talk it through with the group.

3.4 MY LIFE PATH SO FAR (PP.136–137)

Share in pairs. The listener can ask questions for clarification, but not as a 'fact-finding' mission!

The different signs could be called anything at all – independence, new job, family, joy, status quo, stagnation; there is no right or wrong direction – they are just possible choices for the future.

A note here about adolescence. The adolescent years herald the deepening of the skills of cognitive abstraction: the ability to make informed hypotheses and to realize that what happens today has consequences for the future. It is important for all of us to pause at times and take stock of where we are and where we have come from and to recognize that we have choices about where we go next. For an adolescent who has low self-esteem this can be a particularly scary thought. You need to ensure in this exercise that each person has at least one positive choice on their signposts. If someone is having difficulty seeing a positive direction remind her that the crossroads is a place where she can pause and reflect; that if any of the signposts are unclear then it is likely that they will become more recognizable as she starts to set more goals for herself; and that just because we choose a certain path to begin with, it doesn't mean we have to stay on it if it is detrimental to our well-being. There is an imagework exercise for exploring life paths. I have not included it here but you may like to experience this for yourself (see Glouberman 2003, pp.173–191).

3.5 SAME AND DIFFERENT (P.138)

Discuss the introduction to this activity sheet and explore the idea that we may do or say things to try and 'fit in'. Explore the benefits and drawbacks of this.

Discuss the point that sometimes we admire traits in others that we already have ourselves, although not necessarily to the same degree. We can also choose to develop certain qualities. You might also bring up the point that sometimes what we *don't* like in others may be a reflection of a similar trait in ourselves.

Making a list of 'things in common' will help participants to identify or clarify their own beliefs, attitudes, preferences, and so on.

3.6 ME, MY FAMILY AND MY COMMUNITY (P.139)

This is another way of exploring self-concept in relation to others and of identifying possible ways in which the dynamics of a group might change. If I were to place myself somewhere different what would happen in the rest of the group? Where would I most like to be? Is this possible? How might I start to work towards this?

Geoff, who was taking part in a stroke rehabilitation group, placed himself on the very edge of the group circle. When asked where he would like to be, he indicated a place just outside the circle. Geoff told us that he felt very much a part of the group but knew that he was making a rapid recovery and that he would soon need to move away from the group support and 'go it alone'.

Martin placed himself in the very centre of the circle for a self-help group. He felt that other group members looked to him as a role model and he enjoyed the opportunity to support others. He expressed anxiety about the possibility of re-positioning himself nearer the edge of the circle as he felt this would indicate that he had lost his purpose in the group.

Confidence that one is of value and significance as a unique individual is one of the most precious possessions which anyone can have. (Storr 1989, p.96)

3.7 SUMMARY (P.140)

See notes for summary sheet in Section 2 (p.67).

Section 4

Self-Awareness

Aims of this section

- to learn the process of focusing

- to deepen awareness of emotions and how we express these

- to explore the use of imagery in helping to create desired feeling 'states'

Information and activity sheets

INFORMATION SHEET 4A: BEING SELF-AWARE (P.142)

This is for discussion in the whole group.

Suggested reading

Kabat-Zinn, J. (1996) *Full Catastrophe Living: How to Cope with Stress, Pain and Illness Using Mindfulness Meditation.* London: Piatkus.

Stevens, J.O. (1989) *Awareness.* London: Eden Grove.

4.1 FOCUSING (PP.143–144)

Focusing can be used for relaxation on a regular basis (see Section 8 'Self- Reliance and Stress Management'). It is also a way of training the mind to leave behind worries and concerns and be more aware of the present moment. Focusing can be done seated or lying down.

Lead the whole group in this exercise. Leave plenty of time at the end for people to share their experiences of focusing.

Encourage participants to ask themselves questions such as:

- What do I tend to think about when my attention is not focused?

- Am I able to redirect my focus of attention?

- Do I find myself worrying about 'getting it right'?

- Do I find the process easy or difficult?

Rather than try to change, stop, or avoid something that you don't like in yourself, it is much more effective to stay with it and become more deeply aware of it.... When you really get in touch with your own experiencing, you will find that change takes place by itself, without your effort or planning. (Stevens 1989, pp.2–3)

INFORMATION SHEET 4B: AWARENESS OF EMOTIONS (P.145)

Discuss how people experience different emotions and how we might suppress our emotions if we think we should be able to cope or it's wrong to show anger or to cry, and so on. When this happens then there is no appropriate action for people to respond to. Others may not realize how we feel and therefore continue to act in ways that reinforce our original emotions.

Young adolescents tend to be very emotionally labile. This may, in part, be due to hormonal changes but is also often due to the fact that they haven't yet built up enough experience to be able to predict how long things will last or to have developed enough successful coping strategies. They may sometimes need 'permission' to feel what they are feeling and assurance that all emotions are valid and that we can learn strategies to reduce the intensity of some of them. Some young people (as well as some adults) are very unaware of what exactly it is that they are feeling or why they are feeling it. If they feel swamped with emotion they may 'shut down' as a self-protection.

For all these reasons, a sensitive, structured exploration of feelings and how we express them needs to be incorporated into any self-esteem course.

4.2 HOW I NORMALLY EXPRESS EMOTIONS (P.146)

Brainstorm emotions first. Remember to include 'feel good' emotions in the list. The activity sheet can then be completed individually and discussed as general points (rather than in relation to a particular person) in the whole group. It is important to discuss what happens as a consequence of the way we choose to express our emotions: how others respond and why; how we feel afterwards, etc.

4.3 STATE MANAGEMENT (PP.147–148)

This is an amalgam of exercises from neurolinguistic programming and imagework.

'Negative' states are quite easy to manufacture! If someone tells me that I will have to introduce myself to a group in a foreign language and I have only a few minutes to learn how to do it, I am sure that I would experience a state of anxiety. If I was then told that I could do it in English if I wished, my anxiety would subside. My anticipation of what might happen if I attempted a foreign language could cause my body to produce an anxiety state! This link between mind and body can also be demonstrated by getting the group to imagine themselves cutting a slice of lemon and then sucking on it. If you elaborate the picture enough – 'Imagine that you can see the spurt of lemon juice as you slice into the lemon', etc. – the majority of the group will undoubtedly experience a rush of saliva or will indicate a sense of the sour taste by their facial expression.

The unconscious mind believes the images that we form of ourselves as if they were already reality. If we can 'manufacture' a positive experience and make it vivid enough in our imagination then we generally start to act in the real world as though the desired change had already taken place.

I suggest that you demonstrate the state management exercise with just one person from the group and then invite the group to facilitate each other in pairs. It is important to encourage peer facilitation as early as possible in the course to reinforce the idea that individuals will be able to use these exercises on their own or with another group member after the course has finished.

4.4 SUMMARY (P.149)

See notes for summary sheet in Section 2 (p.67).

Section 5

The Challenge of Change

Aims of this section

- to explore the meaning of change in our lives

- to heighten awareness of what helps individuals to make positive changes and of some of the obstacles to change

- to highlight the possibilities of making informed choices about the direction of change

Information and activity sheets

INFORMATION SHEET 5A: DEFINITIONS AND DESCRIPTIONS (P.151)

To be discussed in the group.

Discuss the link between imagework and personal construct theory: imagery can encapsulate constructs and their links remarkably effectively. Images often allow much greater insight than words ever could, and imagework also provides the opportunity to elaborate alternatives, thereby facilitating the process of conscious choice and the possibility of altering our less helpful constructs about ourselves and the world.

Suggested reading

Glouberman, D. (2003) *Life Choices, Life Changes: Develop Your Personal Vision with Imagework.* London: Hodder and Stoughton.

Fransella, F. and Dalton, P. (1990) *Personal Construct Counselling in Action.* London: Sage.

5.1 WHAT IS CHANGE? (P.152–153)

Compare and discuss differing views of change highlighted by the free association exercise. Here are a few examples of how this works:

change – make different – alter – irrevocable – for life

change – different – not the same – unique – a one off – special – stands out from the crowd

change – not the same any more – loss – sadness – yearning – stuck

change – relief – excitement – enthusiasm – energy – leap

5.2 COPING WITH CHANGE (P.154)

Collate any general themes that have been identified.

5.3 MOTIVATION FOR CHANGE (P.155)

Again, this could form the basis for discussion about what motivates different people.

5.4 KEEP IT OR CHANGE IT? (P.156)

This activity sheet could be used as the basis for each group member to take two minutes to 'sell' themselves to the group. The group could also hold an 'auction' of their greatest talents. Encourage use of advertising 'jargon' to make this a fun exercise. I have also used this idea towards the end of a course to have a 'bargain basement' sale of unwanted or now outdated elements.

5.5 MAKING A COMMITMENT (P.157)

Imagining that you have already achieved a goal can be more powerful than planning what you will have to do beforehand. Athletes are often trained to visualize themselves having made the perfect high jump, achieved their personal best time, and so on. This theme is revisited several times in different sections.

5.6 OBSTACLES IN THE WAY OF CHANGE (P.158) AND INFORMATION SHEET 5B: RESISTING CHANGE (P.159)

The aim here is to help participants to recognize that there are very real reasons why change might be difficult. Building self-esteem involves tackling some of these obstacles but also involves recognition that their purpose was self-protection. When we can see the reasons for resistance to change, we are in a better position to be able to choose more useful strategies for looking after ourselves; strategies that will support the change process rather than hinder it (see Part I, Chapter 2, 'Self-Esteem and the Process of Change').

5.7 WORKING ON AVOIDANCES (P.160)

Avoidance is fed by fear, and fear is increased by avoidance! Most people need to work on their avoidances in a structured way so that they feel that each step is manageable. See also Section 11 'Setting and Achieving Goals'.

INFORMATION SHEET 5C: DESENSITIZATION (P.161)

For discussion in the whole group.

5.8 DESENSITIZATION (P.162)

At this point you could introduce the idea of group members suggesting small challenges for each other.

5.9 TAKING RISKS (P.163)

Discuss risks that participants have taken in the past, both large and small. Every change involves a risk of some sort. Some suggestions for minimizing the difficulties involved in taking a risk might be:

- Invest time in researching the risk
- Only tackle one risk at a time
- Start with small goals
- Believe in yourself
- Believe that the risk is worth taking
- Seek support from someone who has already taken a similar risk
- Resolve to accept the worst should it occur
- Do everything possible to make sure that the worst doesn't happen.

5.10 THE ABC OF CHANGE (PP.164–165)

This model comes from Personal Construct Therapy. It is a technique originally outlined by Finn Tschudi (Dalton & Dunnett 1990). It can be demonstrated as a group decision-making process. For example, you could explore the pros and cons of using a regular relaxation technique. The following is an example explored by a group of adults who stammer.

A1 Stammering openly, no techniques used	A2 Using some form of fluency control
Disadvantages	**Advantages**
1. Can lead to frustration if attitude to stammering does not change	1. Gives another option (more choice)
2. Feeling out of control	2. Helps to keep a focus on what you're doing
3. Increased avoidance (unless attitude changes)	3. Increased fluency
4. Difficult to set goal	4. Feel as though 'dealing' with the problem
5. Affects confidence	5. Helps to expand 'comfort zone'
6. Reinforces stammering behaviour?	6. Helps reduce avoidances
	7. Helps you to feel more positive
	8. Can set goals related to process
Advantages	**Disadvantages**
1. If more relaxed about stammering can keep things in perspective	1. Focusing on fluency techniques could 'take over' life
2. Tolerance of occasional stammers and feeling that coped well with these can increase self-esteem and confidence	2. Pressure to keep up the 'front' of being a fluent person all the time
3. Showing that you accept it will get positive reactions from others	3. Becoming reliant on it as a prop
4. Stammer becomes more relaxed when not fighting it or trying to cover it up	4. Hard work. Lots of thinking time
5. Less effort in terms of time needed to 'practise'	5. Fitting the practise into a busy life (i.e. not keeping it in perspective)
	6. Intolerance of occasional stammers could lead to more anxiety

5.11 SUMMARY (P.166)

See notes for summary sheet in Section 2 (p.67).

Section 6

Self-Acceptance

Aims of this section

- to help participants to see that they make sense exactly as they are

- to highlight the difference between self-approval and self-acceptance

- to explore how our thoughts affect the way we feel and act

- to identify unhelpful patterns of thinking

- to appreciate skills and helpful beliefs

Information and activity sheets

INFORMATION SHEET 6A: THE VICIOUS CYCLE (P.168)

Demonstrate with a 'negative' thought identified by the group.

6.1 CHALLENGING YOUR BELIEFS (P.169)

Beliefs that lower self-esteem might be such things as 'it's a family pattern', 'it's all down to fate', 'I can't make small talk', 'I'm the only person I know who can't do this'.

Beliefs that raise self-esteem might be 'I am in control of my own destiny', 'my achievements are due to my hard work, not just luck', 'my opinions are worth listening to'.

One belief is entered in each part of the wheel. The wheel helps you to go where you want to go in life. Beliefs that lower self-esteem cause the wheel to buckle or throw it off balance so you don't get where you want.

This image could be extended into talking about what tools are needed if a 'lowering' thought has buckled the wheel slightly. Perhaps some people can cope with a slight buckling and still get where they want, but at a slower pace. Maybe some repairs need to be made, perhaps some spokes need to be replaced completely. If the wheel keeps taking you off course what needs to be done?

6.2 SOME COMMON PATTERNS OF SELF-TALK THAT LOWER SELF-ESTEEM (P.170)

Having looked at beliefs, participants are now asked to identify any specific 'self-talk' phrases that they use. In many instances, of course, we may not confine these patterns to internal dialogues; we may tell other people these things as though they were indisputable facts!

One teenage group I worked with likened positive thoughts to healthy eating and unhelpful thoughts to eating 'junk' food. They managed to take this metaphor to its limit, describing the gruesome effects that too much junk food/junk thinking might have on your body! Because they had come up with the mind/body link on their own this proved to be a very effective exercise in enabling them to see the relevance of positive self-talk.

Self-talk patterns	Examples
I know what you think (otherwise known as mind-reading!)	You obviously think I don't know what I'm doing.
Total disaster (catastrophizing difficult events)	My whole world will fall apart if I don't know anyone at the party.
These things always go together (if 'a' happens then 'b' ALWAYS follows)	If I book a holiday something is bound to go wrong – it always does.
Everyone and always (overgeneralizing)	Everyone always thinks I'm stupid.
Compared to you	I can never match up to what anyone else can do.

Self-talk patterns	Examples
I should (it is an unwritten law from somewhere)	I will feel guilty/will somehow be punished if I don't do this/feel this.
I must	I don't have any choices. This is the only option.
The whole of me	I am so useless – my boss didn't even say good morning to me.
The world says	It is generally known that… It is believed to be true…
I blame the cat	The cat/teacher/neighbour makes me feel inferior.
Vaguely speaking	It's all down to fate.

6.3 ANALYSIS OF A DIFFICULT SITUATION (P.171)

An example:

My difficult situation is: I have to drive on my own to a meeting.

My usual thoughts are:

I might get lost. The car might break down and I won't know what to do. I'll be late and everyone will think I'm stupid.

How this affects me emotionally:

I feel anxious long before the time I have to go.

I can change these to:

I'll plan my route the day before. I've got my mobile. If I'm late I'll be able to explain.

Emotionally I will feel:

more confident because I will have planned what to do.

81

How this affects me physically:

I get tense. I can't concentrate properly. I end up with a headache.

Physically I will feel:

more relaxed, more able to concentrate.

How this affects my behaviour:

I don't get what I should out of the meeting because I'm so wound up. I end up being short-tempered with people when I get home.

How this will affect my behaviour:

I will enjoy the meeting more. I'll listen to some music on the way back home and arrive back feeling more calm.

6.4 APPRECIATION (P.172)

It may be difficult for some people to appreciate the skills that they have or to see the relevance of these skills in different areas of their lives.

In order to complete the jigsaw, each person thinks of at least three things that they enjoy doing. They then think about what 'skill' or personality trait (asset) they have that enables them to enjoy this pastime. Each 'asset' is entered in the jigsaw. Discuss how many of these could be used when tackling a problem in a different area of life.

> *Sandip enjoys football. In his jigsaw he wrote: co-ordination, agility, team player, determination, dedication, fitness, quick to learn, strategist, risk taker, not afraid to get hurt. During the group discussion he quickly came to see how he could transfer some of these assets to working on his difficulty with his speech.*

Finish the exercise by encouraging participants to appreciate their greatest achievements. Emphasize that these are personal achievements, not achievements compared with anyone else. It may be an achievement for someone to enter a room full of strangers on their own and manage to stay for ten minutes.

6.5 WORK IN PROGRESS (P.173)

A reminder that we don't need to have completed a task before we can start to feel good about ourselves. This also highlights the point that awareness of difficulties doesn't have to be an opportunity to give ourselves even more of a hard time! We need to accept that there will always be things that we will be working on to some degree.

6.6 CONFIDENCE (P.174) AND 6.7 RECREATING A MEMORY (P.175)

These activities provide further opportunities for the group to facilitate each other after a demonstration. Sometimes people worry that the first of these exercises isn't 'real', that guessing how someone else might feel when they are confident won't help them to be confident in real life. It's important to explore the idea that we all 'act' in different ways according to who we are with and according to the situation – even something as simple as the difference between watching a scary film at the cinema and watching it in the privacy of your own home can demonstrate this (for some people!). Acting 'as if' we were someone else for a short period simply gives us the opportunity to explore how things would be if we chose to act differently: it highlights that we do have a choice in how we think and behave.

See also state management exercise (activity sheet 4.3) and activity sheet 3.5.

6.8 SUMMARY (P.176)

See notes for summary sheet in Section 2 (p.67).

Self and Others

Aims of this section

- to reflect on how low self-esteem can affect how we behave in relationships

- to think about individual rights within relationships

- to explore issues of assertive and non-assertive communication

Information and activity sheets

INFORMATION SHEET 7A: SELF-ESTEEM WITHIN A RELATIONSHIP (P.178)

For discussion in the whole group. Devise a possible 'vicious cycle' together, using an example offered by a group member if possible.

Although every relationship will have its difficulties, this may be hard to accept for those who have idealized views of friendships and intimate relationships. A 'healthy' relationship might be defined as one where each person has a secure, defined sense of self and is therefore able to let the other person be separate, rather than one looking to the other to fulfil their needs. This secure sense of self will have its origins in early childhood experiences and the capacity to rely on internal processes for one's own sense of self-worth. The ability to 'merge' with another without feeling 'swamped' or restricted relies on learning to differentiate self from others and learning about our own boundaries. It also involves being sure of our ability to reclaim boundaries if they are temporarily and voluntarily dissolved, as often happens when people 'fall in love'.

> Every interaction between two people has a powerful impact on the respective worth of each and what happens between them. (Satir 1991, p.58)

7.1 GETTING A BROADER PERSPECTIVE (P.179)

At the point of imagining a conversation with the friend, encourage participants actually to move into another seat when they are 'being' that person.

I first experienced this exercise during a counselling skills workshop. We each had to think of a teenager with whom we were finding some difficulty. When we stepped into the shoes of the teenagers the atmosphere around the room changed very noticeably as people tried to feel what it must be like to be their teenage sons, daughters or clients! People gained some valuable insights that day and several of us reported changes in how we handled the situation we were exploring.

7.2 SOME QUESTIONS FOR DISCUSSION (P.180)

If numbers permit, divide the group up so that different groups discuss each one of the suggested questions. Draw together the responses in the large group again.

7.3 THE HOUSE OF RELATIONSHIPS (P.181–182)

The house of relationships is adapted from an exercise on health and illness by Dina Glouberman (2003, pp.226–227).

INFORMATION SHEET 7B: WHAT IS ASSERTIVENESS? (P.183)

Because issues of self-esteem are so multifaceted, I strongly believe that assertiveness training should not be undertaken in isolation, as if it were a 'method' for building self-esteem all of its own. This is one of the reasons why I have included it as part of an overall section on self-esteem within relationships. It could just as easily have been placed in several of the other sections and this is worth pointing out to groups.

Assertiveness guidelines help us to take a problem-solving approach to life's challenges. I don't generally refer to assertive communication as using 'techniques' and I have tried to emphasize this on the relevant sheets. These are guidelines to support individuals while they establish for themselves what it is to enjoy open and honest communication with others.

I have included brief definitions of non-assertive behaviour here as these are widely known in the context of assertiveness training. However, I have found Virginia Satir's outline of different communication patterns very useful as a discussion point in groups (see next activity sheet). You might find it useful to explore the links between these two approaches with your group.

7.4 THE CHOCOLATE DEBATE (P.184)

(I am grateful to Marsha Lomond, a psychotherapist and fellow imagework practitioner, who taught me the chocolate debate exercise in the context of a different set of roles.)

Family therapist Virginia Satir identified four common communication patterns when self-esteem is threatened:

> Whenever there was any stress, over and over again I observed four ways people had of handling it. These four patterns occurred only when one was reacting to stress *and at the same time* felt his self-esteem was involved. (Satir 1991, p.59)

The four patterns of communication are: *placating, blaming, computing* and *distracting.* All these are non-assertive communication patterns.

Divide the group into fours. Any extras should act as observers throughout the whole exercise. Explain that each person will have the chance to play all four roles and that these roles are to be played 'to the extreme'. Explain the roles as follows:

- *Placater.* Doesn't want to 'rock the boat' or upset anyone in any way so will tend to agree with everything and try to make everyone happy. Takes the blame for everything, apologizes frequently.

- *Blamer.* Finds fault with everything and blames everyone else for whatever goes wrong; will use words like 'why do you always…' and 'you never do…'. The blamer is aiming to appear 'strong' when actually they are feeling low in self-worth.

- *Computer.* Cool, calm and collected. Tends to use long words in order to sound as though she really knows what she is talking about. Will often refer to something she has read on the subject. Appears 'without emotion', quite detached and very still (no expressive hand gestures!).

- *Distracter.* Whatever the distracter does or says is irrelevant to whatever else is going on because he feels out of place. He is constantly moving around and fidgeting. He asks questions or makes comments that have nothing to do with the topic being discussed.

The group are to imagine that they are having a family discussion about chocolate. Actual position in the family (mother, father, child, aunt, etc.) is not relevant here. Each group sits in a circle. Everyone has just one minute in each role. At the end of the minute everyone moves round one chair to the left and assumes the next role. (If you have several groups doing this it can get quite loud and I have had to resort to ringing a Tibetan bell at times to indicate the end of the minute!)

This is a high-energy, fun activity but it can bring up all sorts of feelings and recognition of patterns in self and others. It is crucial to give everyone the chance to de-role at the end of the exercise. Participants can do this by swapping chairs again and talking about what they are going to do that evening or what they had for breakfast.

Make sure there is still plenty of time left in the session to talk about how people experienced this and to reinforce the idea that behaviour patterns are not written in stone!

Satir identifies a fifth communication pattern, which she calls *levelling*. A leveller communicates openly and honestly and their body language matches what they are saying and thinking:

Of the five responses only the leveling one has any chance to heal ruptures, break impasses, or build bridges between people. And lest leveling seems too unrealistic to you, let me assure you that you can still placate if you choose, blame if you like, be on a head trip, or be distracting. The difference is you know what you are doing and are prepared to take the consequences for it. (Satir 1991, p.73)

7.5 BEING HEARD (P.185)

For discussion in pairs.

7.6 ASSERTIVE REQUESTS (P.186)

Think about your body language. Does the person's body language reflect assertiveness? You could refer back to the chocolate debate and talk about the different postures and actions used in the four patterns of communication during that exercise.

Set the scene. This also refers to choosing the appropriate time and place.

Use 'I' statements. Take responsibility for how you are feeling. Remind participants of the communication guidelines discussed at the start of the course.

Be clear about the separateness between you and others. A reminder that we can alter the way that we react to people. We don't need to feel stuck in certain ways of being, even if the other person remains unchanged.

Be specific in your requests and ask the other person to be specific too. This is worth practising in the group. Ask everyone to come up with an assertive request for three different situations. These requests should specify actions very clearly, e.g. 'I would appreciate your help washing up the coffee mugs next Thursday evening after the meeting' (rather than 'You never bother to help clear up after the meeting'). Encourage awareness of intonation patterns! This is a simple request not an accusation!

Acknowledge the other person's point of view (empathize). For example, 'I can see that you thought I didn't mind doing the clearing up, but I'd find it helpful if you did the coffee mugs while I'm clearing up the kitchen.'

Keep an eye on your common goals. 'We both want to keep the place tidy for other people.'

Stay with your statement. Avoid allowing your self-esteem to be 'hooked'. 'I don't enjoy doing all the chores on a Thursday. I'd find it helpful if you did the coffee mugs.'

7.7 SAYING 'NO' (P.187)

Invite the group (in pairs) to try out different ways of saying 'no' to an unreasonable request without being direct. Discuss how it felt to be on the receiving end of an indirect 'no'.

Identify several unreasonable requests that could be role played in the group.

Encourage participants to try easy 'nos' first and to save the more difficult situations until they have had several successes with the easy ones.

7.8 COPING WITH CRITICISM (P.188)

Again, people need to try this out in the group. Participants may have had recent experience of being criticized and could devise an assertive response and try it out in role play with one other person. Otherwise, you will need a few possible scenarios ready for people to try.

It is, of course, important not to sound challenging when asking for examples or further explanation: 'I'd find it helpful if you could give me some examples of what you mean.'

Discuss other strategies that participants have tried that they feel have worked for them.

7.9 GIVING FEEDBACK TO SOMEONE ELSE (P.189)

Rather than providing the guidelines here, this is an opportunity for group members to come up with their own ideas based on the skills they have already identified and practised.

7.10 GIVING AND RECEIVING PRAISE AND COMPLIMENTS (P.190)

Emphasize appropriateness and sincerity in giving praise and compliments. It is best to look at the other person in a relaxed way; be sincere; use 'I' statements and be specific.

7.11 SUMMARY (P.191)

See notes for summary sheet in Section 2 (p.67).

Section 8

Self-Reliance and Stress Management

Aims of this section

- to help participants to identify any stress factors in their lives

- to identify personal reactions to stress

- to demonstrate the possibility of using positive self-help strategies to deal with stress

Information and activity sheets

INFORMATION SHEET 8A: STRESS MANAGEMENT (P.193)

For discussion in the whole group.

8.1 IDENTIFICATION (P.194)

This could be a 'do at home' activity given out at the end of the last session on 'self-esteem in relationships'.

INFORMATION SHEET 8B THE STRESS REACTION (P.195)

For discussion in the whole group.

Suggested Reading

Madders, J. (1987) *Stress and Relaxation.* London: Macdonald Optima.

8.2 PHYSICAL SIGNS (P.196)

Encourage the group to share their experiences of stress reactions and find common patterns.

Particular emphasis should be placed on the connection between lowered self-esteem and stress reactions.

INFORMATION SHEET 8C: RECOGNIZING THE SIGNS OF STRESS (P.197)

Again, the link between thoughts and physical responses (mind and body) can be emphasized. Some of these symptoms can obviously occur for medical reasons and may have nothing to do with stress. Participants need to be aware that we are simply looking at *possible* ways in which stress might affect us physically.

8.3 WHAT CAN YOU DO TO COPE WITH EVERYDAY STRESS? (P.198)

This could be discussed in pairs. Listeners may be tempted to make suggestions as to what the other person should do in order to balance out his or her days. Pre-empt this by reminding everyone that what works for one person may not work for another, and that the idea is to come up with your own solutions.

8.4 ENJOYMENT (PP.199–200)

This could well take up a whole session on its own! All the points can be discussed in the whole group. Encourage everyone to come up with at least one thing that they will definitely do before the next meeting to bring some more joy into their lives.

You could incorporate an imagery exercise here such as 'Future me!' (activity sheet 2.2). Questions you could ask for the positive future are:

- What is your diet like?
- What do you do to maintain a healthy sleep pattern?
- What physical activity do you do?
- What form of relaxation do you use?
- How do you manage your time?

Share responses in the group after the exercise so that participants can pool useful strategies.

Spend some time planning a 'perfect day out'. See if there's anything that anyone could actually do from this during the next week.

8.5 WORRY CRUNCHING (P.201)

Brainstorm other effective 'worry crunchers'. Invite everyone to take one idea to try out before the next meeting. You could do this as a 'lucky dip' exercise. Write each type of worry cruncher on pieces of paper (it doesn't matter if you have to repeat some). Everyone takes one from 'the hat' and experiments with the idea during the coming week. If they really don't have any worries during the week, they could offer the idea to a friend or relative to try out if they want to!

8.6 PROCRASTINATING AND PRIORITIZING (P.202)

Suggested reading: Perry, A. (2002) *Isn't It About Time? How to Stop Putting Things Off and Get On with Your Life.* London: Worth Publishing.

8.7 POSTURE (P.203)

Discuss this in pairs. Point out any common patterns in the whole group.

8.8 BREATHING PATTERNS (P.204) AND INFORMATION SHEET 8D INSPIRATION AND EXPIRATION (P.205)

For discussion in the whole group.

8.9 USING ABDOMINAL BREATHING FOR STRESS MANAGEMENT (P.206)

Based on a simple meditation technique, focusing on breathing can be effective in reducing feelings of stress, even for those who suffer from panic attacks. Although thinking about breathing may be difficult at first, it is a very positive way of increasing awareness of what relaxed breathing feels like.

INFORMATION SHEETS 8E: RELAXING YOUR BODY (P.207) AND 8F: RELAXING EFFECTIVELY (P.208)

You will find a selection of relaxation scripts in the appendices to this book.

Suggested reading

Kabat-Zinn, J. (1996) *Full Catastrophe Living: How to Cope with Stress, Pain and Illness Using Mindfulness Meditation.* London: Piatkus.

8.10 DIARY NOTES (P.209) AND 8.11 RELAXATION SCORE SHEET (P.210)

These can be used to encourage self-monitoring both during and after the course.

8.12 ACTION PLAN (P.211)

Discuss goals in pairs or in the whole group to encourage people to be as specific as possible.

8.13 IMAGINE A MIRACLE! (P.212)

The 'miracle question' has its origins in a conversation between a therapist and a client at the Brief Family Therapy Centre in Milwaukee:

Therapist: How will you know when things are better?

Client: That would take a miracle.

Therapist: OK, suppose a miracle had happened...

For this exercise, the format of the question has been adapted to incorporate elements of imagework. Quite frequently, people have told me that they notice themselves doing things the next morning 'as if' the miracle had happened.

8.14 SUMMARY (P.213)

See notes for summary sheet in Section 2 (p.67).

Section 9

Self-Expression

Aims of this section

- to explore the main elements of successful social communication

- to allow participants the opportunity to devise some useful strategies for social interaction

- to continue to reinforce the mind/body link

Information and activity sheets

9.1 SOCIAL SKILLS (P.215)

The main elements to encourage participants to think about are:

- understanding and using non-verbal communication successfully

- questioning

- opening and closing a conversation

- listening

- maintaining a conversation.

9.2 PYRAMIDING (P.216)

This is based on an exercise from Personal Construct Therapy. Start by asking the group to think of someone they know who they consider to be socially skilled. Identify three or four examples of behaviour that indicate that a person is socially skilled. Take each of these in turn and identify even more specifically what the elements of this behaviour are, refining the behaviours into smaller and smaller units. At the end of the exercise you will have identified some specific behaviours that participants can choose to incorporate into their social interactions. It is hoped they will also have recognized many aspects that they are already doing. This is an example of a pyramid of communication skills from a speech and language therapy group:

Successful Communication

can put across ideas clearly — **Interesting to listen to** — 'straight forward' — friendly — considerate

precise (not rambling) — sharing a common interest — **Good listener** — asks questions especially 'open ended' — knows when to stop — appropriate facial expression — interested in others

eye contact — **Body language** — facial expression — **Verbal response**

tension/ relaxation — general posture — head movements — **Timing** — comments agreeing/disagreeing — not interrupting too much — fillers e.g. Mmm

uses pauses — asking and waiting — picking up signals — noting feedback (response)

9.3 EYE CONTACT (P.217)

For discussion in the whole group.

9.4 STARTING A CONVERSATION (P.218)

Encourage the group to devise their own examples for each of the guidelines given on the activity sheet.

Use open-ended rather than closed questions:

> I heard you had a great holiday. What did you do?

Notice and respond to any new information:

Speaker: I thought I was going to be late. I'm not used to the buses here.

Listener: Are you new to the area?

Offer some information about yourself and see if it's picked up:

> I sometimes use the bus too. I really enjoy not having to drive at weekends.

Brainstorm different ways that people initiate conversation. This is also a good 'do at home' task. Participants can be asked to observe precisely what friends and family (or characters from soap operas!) do and say to initiate conversation and then report back to the group.

9.5 LISTENING SKILLS (P.219) AND 9.6 MAINTAINING RAPPORT (P.220)

Effective listening skills should include:

- showing interest by using appropriate facial expression and body language

- not interrupting

- not changing the topic

- asking appropriate questions to clarify if necessary

- keeping relaxed eye contact

- using natural prompts such as 'Mmm', 'Yes', 'I see'

- showing accurate listening by making links between different parts of what the speaker is talking about

- allowing more than brief silences to give the speaker time to think

- picking up on non-verbal cues to better understand what the speaker is feeling.

9.7 PAUSING (P.221)

Why do we pause?

- to give ourselves time to think
- to give the other person time to absorb what we've said
- to take a breath
- because we are filled with emotion
- to emphasize a point
- to maintain a feeling of calmness.

9.8 ENDING A CONVERSATION (P.222)

This could also be used for a 'do at home' observation task before discussion in the group.

9.9 IMAGINE IT AGAIN! (P.223)

This task is aimed at further reinforcing the idea of state management. See activity sheet 4.3.

9.10 SUMMARY (P.224)

See notes for summary sheet in Section 2 (p.67).

Section 10

Creative Problem-Solving

Aims of this session

- to explore a variety of methods for problem-solving

- to encourage awareness of existing skills in problem-solving

Information and activity sheets

INFORMATION SHEET 10A: CREATIVE PROBLEM-SOLVING (P.226)

Einstein was famously creative in the way he used images to experiment with ideas and to solve problems:

> Leaps of imaginative ideas, which need not be at all logical to begin with, seem to be essential to any new departure, in science as anywhere else... For instance, Einstein made one of his great leaps toward the theory of relativity when he was about sixteen and carried out one of his 'thought experiments'. This was to imagine himself as a particle of light traveling away from a planet at the speed of light, and then looking back at the planet thinking how it would appear. (Rayner 1993, pp.146–147)

10.1 HOW DO YOU NORMALLY SET ABOUT SOLVING PROBLEMS? (P.227)

Possible scenarios to suggest to the group:

- You want to raise money for Red Nose Day but the group is having difficulty coming up with a workable idea.

- A child in your family is being bullied at school.

- You work in the clothing industry and your boss has asked you to come up with some ideas for a new range of products that will appeal to the teenage market.

- You have been given the task of arranging a 'special' party for a good friend but you have a limited budget.

- You have to give a five-minute talk at an evening class you attend and you're not sure how to plan it out.

- You want to change your usual routine so that you have time to fit in an evening class twice a week.

10.2 WHAT SKILLS ARE INVOLVED IN PROBLEM-SOLVING? (P.228)

Can you tie a knot in a piece of string without letting go of either end? The trick is to cross your arms before picking up the string!

Can you draw a dot inside a circle without taking your pen off the paper? Fold the corner of the page. Draw a dot at the tip of the folded corner. Draw a line towards the fold and then start to draw a circle across the fold. Open up the paper without taking your pen off and complete the circle.

Another well-known problem of this sort is the problem of the nine dots:

.   .   .

.   .   .

.   .   .

The task is to connect all the dots using four straight lines and without taking your pen off the paper. The solution is to extend the lines that you draw beyond the imaginary square that you first see in the pattern of dots.

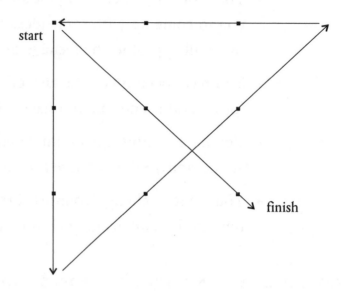

This sort of task highlights the notion that for some problems we may need to look beyond our usual way of thinking and think 'outside the box'. I remember being shown this as a child – it can be very frustrating when you are trying to work it out, and yet seems so obvious once you know how. But isn't that the way sometimes with some of our problems?!

10.3 PROBLEM FOCUSED OR SOLUTION FOCUSED? (PP.229–230)

This could be facilitated as an imagery exercise, by asking participants to imagine themselves as though they were actually in the situation again. In this instance, instead of projecting forward to a time when a problem has been solved you are inviting participants to recall a time when they've already used effective skills. They can then be encouraged to think about how any of these skills might be useful for tackling a current difficulty.

10.4 MORE EXAMPLES (P.231)

Encourage participants to use one or more methods to try and solve a long-standing (but not major) problem and to report back on how things went.

10.5 USING IMAGERY (P.232)

This is adapted from the 'Image as metaphor' exercise by Dina Glouberman (2003, pp.94–116).

10.6 USING DRAWING (PP.233–235)

Drawing is another way of accessing the subconscious and of utilizing the right side of the brain.

Drawing can be used to explore situations and questions by people who usually rely heavily on words and logic just as easily as by those who cannot find the words to describe and explore difficulties as they would like. In a similar way to using visual images in our minds, drawing can also be used to look at different aspects of the same thing and to create links between present and future. This is an exercise I was shown at a workshop run by Tom Ravenette, who used drawing extensively in his work as an educational psychologist. 'A drawing and its opposite' may reveal something about the artist that he or she had not thought of before.

10.7 SUMMARY (P.236)

See notes for summary sheet in Section 2 (p.67).

Section 11

Setting and Achieving Goals

Aims of this section

- to reflect again on some of the obstacles to making changes and setting goals

- to explore some possible goals for the future

- to understand the importance of creating hierarchies

Information and activity sheets

INFORMATION SHEET 11A: SETTING AND ACHIEVING GOALS (P.238)

A person who sets regular goals and is ready and able to evaluate his progress on an ongoing basis will find that he has a sense of direction and purpose and can accomplish more in a short period. It is useful to set ourselves a mixture of short-, medium- and long-term goals. Too many long-term goals may be disheartening if there are no short-term ones to keep us motivated.

11.1 IF I WASN'T WAITING (P.239)

This is a potentially 'high energy' exercise that is an easy one to do in pairs.

11.2 GUIDING PRINCIPLES (P.240)

See Part I, Chapter 2, 'Self-Esteem and the Process of Change'.

11.3 AN EXAMPLE OF USING IMAGERY FOR GOAL-SETTING (P.241)

You could lead the whole group in this exercise, or if there is anyone in the group who already feels confident enough to facilitate this they could try it at home first and then lead the group at the next session.

Leave plenty of time after the exercise to let people talk about their drawings. Remind the group that we cannot interpret anyone else's drawings for them.

11.4 TAKING STEPS (PP.242–243)

This is another way of building hierarchies. As it is quite a lengthy activity it is best demonstrated with one person before participants pair up to facilitate each other.

As noted before, imagery can be used very effectively in goal-setting by providing an opportunity to project yourself forward in time in your imagination and see a positive outcome, experiencing it in as much detail as possible and, in effect, creating a memory of the event as if it had already happened. This forward projection allows you the chance to recognize where you are at the moment – how far along the road you have already come and also to discover some of the things that you will need to know in order to achieve your goal. Perhaps other people will need to be involved and you can visualize how this might come about. You can also explore some of the things that might hinder you, things that you will have to overcome in order to achieve your goal.

11.5 BEING EFFECTIVE (P.244–245)

Discuss the process with the group. When everyone has decided on a goal, give plenty of time for them to facilitate each other in threes. The third person can offer reminders of the process if the person facilitating wants some extra support. This could again be quite lengthy. Allow at least 45–60 minutes so that all three people have a chance at working on their goal and facilitating someone else.

11.6 SUMMARY (P.246)

Make sure that everyone has time during the session to make notes on their summary sheet and to state their positive intention aloud in the group.

Section 12

Keeping It All Going!

Aims of this section

- to review the course
- to identify resources for the future
- to celebrate achievements

12.1 A REVIEW OF BELIEFS, THOUGHTS AND ACTIONS (PP.248–249)

Participants mark the ones they feel they are still working on or need to remind themselves about.

12.2 SUSTAINING THE CHANGES (P.250)

Successful self-prompts might be charts on the wall, reminders on the mirror, notes on your desk at work, drawings of images, small figures of images (I have used plastic animals, for example).

12.3 COPING WITH SETBACKS (P.251) AND 12.4 WHAT WORKS FOR YOU? (P.252)

Both these activities are also useful for a follow-up session once the group members have had a chance to 'go it alone' for a while.

12.5 FEELING INSPIRED? (P.253)

You could either take in a collection of sayings for people to choose from or set this as a task for the group to do before the last session. I also like to ask group members to bring in any other relevant literature, course information, website addresses, and so on, that they think might be interesting for the rest of the group to know about.

12.6 LETTER FROM THE EXPERT (P.254)

If appropriate for the group that you are running, you may want to provide stamped envelopes and offer to post these letters to participants at some point in the future. Leave at least two or three weeks before sending them.

At the end of the course ask each participant to write a short 'appreciation' for everyone else. This is simply done by having one piece of paper for each person passed around the group. Participants read the sheet before they leave but, if they want you to, you could add these appreciations to each person's letter from the expert. It can be a great boost to receive praise like this a few weeks after the course has finished.

12.7 FINISHING THE COURSE (P.255)

Allow time for people to complete this during the session and still leave enough time for your closing circle and end of course celebration.

Part III

Information and Activity Sheets

Section 1

Getting Started

Information sheet 1A

Introduction

This course has been designed to help you to help yourself. The activity sheets and discussion topics will provide you with the opportunity to explore different aspects of self-esteem and to begin to make the changes that you want.

Here are some important points to keep in mind as you make a start:

- We all have the ability to solve problems and to make effective changes in our lives. Sometimes we need to remind ourselves of how to do this.

- Change of any sort affects us on all levels. For example, a change in the way that you think about a certain situation can lead to changes in how you feel physically and in how you behave in that situation.

- When you feel 'stuck', if you take note of what the 'whole' of you is feeling, thinking and sensing then you are likely to come up with some creative solutions to your difficulties.

- A self-esteem course of this type can help you to feel more in control of your life and to enjoy more fulfilling relationships; it won't necessarily help you to be more healthy, wealthy or famous! (But if it does, the author would like to hear about it!)

1.1 Getting to know the group

Find as many people as possible in the group who can agree with the following statements. Write their names in the space provided.

I own a bicycle (and I use it)

I have a pet

I enjoy watching sport

I have seen one of my favourite films more than three times

I like spicy food

It took me more than one hour to get here today

I play a musical instrument

I have an unusual hobby

I don't like chocolate

1.2 Remembering names

Names are an important part of who we are. You may have chosen to shorten your name or use a nickname to reflect how you would like to be known. Remembering other people's names is an important skill and there are many techniques that can help you to do this. One is to associate the person's name with something else – an object, something they like doing, a colour they like to wear and so on. For each person in the group, note down something that will help you to remember his or her name.

Group Members

Name	Memory aid

1.3 Being part of a group

Throughout life most of us have the chance to be part of many different groups, including family, school, work, sport and friendship groups. You may feel more comfortable in some types of group than others and you will have developed certain ways of 'being' and thinking about yourself in relation to different groups. It is important to recognize that you have some choice about this.

How I normally cope with groups	How I would like to be in this group
What I believe I can contribute to this group	**What would help me to feel most comfortable in this group?**

1.4 Communication guidelines

These guidelines are important for all communications and will be useful to keep in mind throughout the course. When you have discussed them in your group, write what you feel each of these guidelines involves.

Listening accurately

Using 'I', not 'you'

Giving constructive feedback

Recognition of personal values

Looking for the common goal

1.5 Feelings and expectations

If you have the determination to follow this course through you will discover that you have a greater degree of control over the way you choose to lead your life and your ability to set and accomplish goals. Take a few moments first to think about where you are starting from.

What are your feelings as you start the course? What do you feel confident about?	What are your expectations of this course? What would you like to know more about?
What would you like to have achieved by the end of this course?	What do you feel are the main obstacles that you will need to overcome?

How You Can Benefit Most From This Course

Keep referring to the course notes

The activity sheets are designed to be used alongside group sessions and also as a resource for self-management following completion of the course. You will gain most benefit if you read through each section several times before moving on to the next part.

Devote specific time to working on your current goals

As well as the time you are involved in the group, it is important that you set aside a short period every day when you are working on one particular goal with your full concentration. You will find that as you become more familiar with the ideas and strategies, they will become a natural part of your daily life. However, devoting a set period every day will ensure that you gain maximum benefit in a shorter time.

Make the course personally relevant

As you go through each activity make sure that you understand every step. Constantly ask yourself what relevance it has to you and how you can apply it to your own life. Make notes as often as you can when thoughts occur to you and when each area is being discussed in your group. Make a point of acting on ideas straight away while they are still fresh in your mind.

Seek support

Discuss this course and the goals you are setting with as many friends and members of your family as possible. This will help you to remember important concepts and is also a major step forward in building your self-esteem. You will, of course, have the support of the group facilitators and other group members, but as you make more and more changes it will be helpful to have support and encouragement from outside the group.

What Is Self-Esteem?

Self-Concept and Self-Esteem

Our *self-concept* is the overall view that we have of ourselves, including our appearance, abilities, attitudes and beliefs.

Our self-concept develops over time and is mostly based on the way in which we interpret the reactions we get from other people. This process begins with our earliest interactions as babies.

Generally, we try to act in a way that fits in with our self-concept. When new information is received to add to our system of beliefs about ourselves we may, therefore, use a process of 'biased filtering'. This means that if the information fits in with our self-concept we will probably accept it as being true. If it doesn't fit in with how we see ourselves then we might ignore it, misinterpret it or reject it completely.

In this way our beliefs affect how we see the world. Even if we have beliefs about ourselves that don't match with reality they are true for us because we believe them to be true.

Self-esteem is about the value we place on ourselves and our abilities. If a person's view of herself (her self-concept) is close to how she would like to be (her 'ideal' self) then she can be said to have healthy self-esteem. An 'ideal' self can be a self who accepts all aspects of her personality and who feels comfortable with who she is. 'Ideal' doesn't have to mean perfect!

We can have different levels of self-esteem in different areas of our lives. These levels can change according to circumstances. For example, self-esteem is often affected when a relationship that was important to us has come to an end.

A person with healthy self-esteem feels OK about being herself while still respecting the needs and feelings of others.

Global and Specific Self-Esteem

Home + School + Social Life + Society

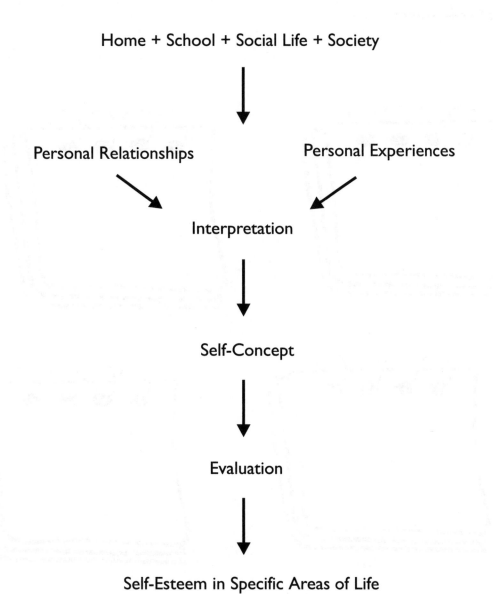

Personal Relationships

Personal Experiences

Interpretation

Self-Concept

Evaluation

Self-Esteem in Specific Areas of Life

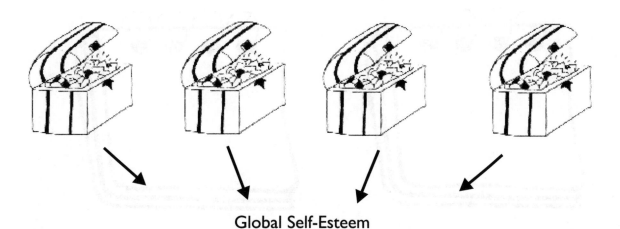

Global Self-Esteem

2.1 Being specific

Think of some different areas in your life where you would like to have a greater feeling of self-esteem

2.2 Future me!

We can't always predict what someone else might say or do (however much we might like to!) but we can be in charge of our own behaviour. Our minds might naturally dwell on negative thoughts but we can use this to our advantage by identifying specific actions and thoughts that we can change in ourselves. In this next exercise you will be able to identify ways in which what you do and what you think influence the outcome of a particular situation. Imagining an event as if it had already happened and imagining both a negative and then a positive outcome in this way can be very powerful.

Look at the previous activity and choose one area of self-esteem that you would like to concentrate on first. Now think of a specific situation which, if tackled success-fully, would boost your self-esteem in this area. For example, the category you choose might be 'being more independent' and a specific situation might be 'making an official phone call confidently'.

Read through the following instructions or have someone read them to you.

When you are ready, close your eyes and relax your body. Imagine that it is the end of the situation you chose. Imagine that things did *not* go well. Ask yourself the following questions:

- What did I do that meant this didn't work well?

- What was I thinking before and during the situation?

- What did I say/not say that meant this didn't go well?

- What was I feeling physically before and during the situation?

- What else do I notice about what happened?

- What is the uncomfortable feeling right now? What is the main thing that makes me feel like this?

- What was the main decision or attitude that got me here?

2.2 (continued)

Now let that image go. Give your body a bit of a shake and then settle back into a relaxed position again. Remember, you are imagining that the event has already happened. This time you are feeling good because things went really well. Ask yourself the following questions:

- Exactly what are the 'good' feelings that I have now?

- What did I personally do that meant that this worked well? What did I do before and during the situation that led to such a positive outcome?

- What was I thinking before and during the situation?

- What did I say/not say?

- How was I feeling?

- What was the main decision or attitude that got me here?

- What else do I notice about what happened?

Remember in all this to use your 'memory' from the future, not your 'thoughts' about what it might be like.

2.3 Expectations

When you are ready, make notes for yourself about what you imagined. Discuss this with one other person in the group. Did you have any thoughts in common?

The situation I chose was:

What I did, thought, said and felt in my negative outcome:

What I did, thought, said and felt in my positive outcome:

What do you think 'self-fulfilling prophecy' means?

2.4 Why is it important to raise our levels of self-esteem?

(Remember, the opposite of low self-esteem is not necessarily high self-esteem. It may be a quiet accepting and liking of yourself – a healthy sense of self-worth and competence.)

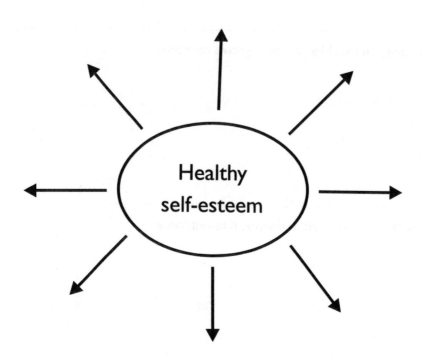

2.5 An image of self-esteem

What is the basic quality of self-esteem for you? Sit quietly for a moment with your eyes closed and allow your imagination to come up with an image that somehow represents what self-esteem means to you. It could be an animal, an object, a plant, a colour – anything at all. Try not to think about this in any logical sense – just allow an image to 'appear' in your mind. Examine this image from all angles. What are its qualities? Now allow your imagination to take one step further – imagine that you can become this image. Step into being the image. As this image, ask yourself the following questions:

- What is it like to be me (the image)?

- What do I feel physically?

- What do I feel emotionally?

- What do I feel mentally?

- What is the best thing about being this image?

- What is the worst thing?

- As this image, what would I most like to happen next?

- What advice do I have for 'self'?

When you are ready, draw or make notes about your image as a reminder of some of the important elements of self-esteem.

2.6 Personal checklist

Shade in the boxes to show how much each of these statements is true for you.

I have a strong sense of who I am	I am very aware of how I behave in different ways according to the situation I am in	I have a good understanding of how different relationships work	I am able to be independent and self-reliant
I am able to be in a relationship without feeling swamped or overwhelmed by the other person	I can usually see things from other people's perspectives	I am usually realistic about how I think others view me	I am respectful and tolerant of other people's views
I understand my emotions and why I feel the way I do in different situations	I feel in control of how I express my emotions	I am able to distinguish my feelings from those of others	I am able to acknowledge my own strengths
I believe that I am a likeable and worthwhile person	I recognize areas that I find difficult and may want to work on	I can accept constructive criticism from others	I am assertive in the way that I deal with unjustified criticism from others
I can tolerate my own mistakes	I like and respect myself	I feel OK about my physical appearance	I take good care of myself

2.6 (continued)

I know how to relax and enjoy myself	I am self-motivated. I tend not to worry too much what others might think of me	I am able to adjust my actions, feelings and thoughts according to realistic assessments of my progress	I believe that I have mastery over my life
I enjoy new challenges	I believe that I let other people see who I really am through my words and actions	I am usually able to listen well to what others have to say	I enjoy talking to new people
I consider myself to be a creative person	I believe that my opinions, thoughts and actions have value	I am confident enough in my own abilities to be able to try different ways of solving problems	I am generally optimistic
I tend not to dwell on past events or worry about the future	I regularly set myself realistic yet challenging goals	I cope well with unexpected events	I believe that I am capable of fulfilling my potential

The Iceberg of Self-Esteem

Many difficulties can be looked at in terms of an 'iceberg'.

There are parts of a difficulty that can be heard and seen.

These *overt* aspects are equivalent to the part of an iceberg that lies above the water.

When a person is coping with a difficulty there are usually many things going on below the surface. These *covert* aspects may include the physical feelings associated with the problem as well as the emotions involved.

Both parts of the iceberg need to be worked on in order to achieve long-term gains.

2.7 My personal iceberg of self-esteem

Overt

_____

Covert

2.8 Summary

What I understand about self-esteem:

What I understand about my own self-esteem:

My positive intention is:

You are now going to spend some time thinking in more detail about your self-concept. Remember, this is the overall view that you have of yourself, including your appearance, abilities, attitudes and beliefs.

Section 3

Who Am I?

3.1 Who am I?

Something important about me	Physical features
Personality	Beliefs
Talents and skills	Things I enjoy
Things I dislike	Important events
Important people	Important places
Difficulties I have overcome	Hopes/ambitions

Anything else?

3.2 Character sketch

Imagine that you are writing a script for a play about your life. How would you describe yourself in a character sketch? Write as though you are your own best friend, someone who knows you better than anyone else and is supporting and understanding of the true you. Start with your name.

_____ is

Now give your play a title:_____

3.3 Imagine that!

Your group leader will talk you through the following imagery exercise when you do it for the first time. These notes are a reminder of the process for when you come to do the same exercise again on your own in the future.

Read through the following instructions and then close your eyes and allow an image to emerge. Just let an image appear in your mind and go with whatever comes for you. Whatever image you get, however ordinary or strange it might be, will have some significance for you if you take the time to explore it.

When you are ready, settle yourself in a comfortable position and allow your eyes to close. Breathe slowly and deeply three times – in through your nose and out through your mouth. Then forget about your breathing.

As your mind and body start to relax, allow an image to emerge that somehow represents who you are. This image could be an animal, an object, a plant or bird or a colour.

When you have an image, allow yourself to explore it as fully as possible. What does it look like, sound like, feel like? If it can move, how does it move? Imagine that you can take a bird's eye view of this image. As you imagine yourself looking down on it from above, notice its relationship to its environment. Is it alone or with others? Does it seem to 'fit' with its surroundings? What else can you notice?

Now imagine that you can actually become this image so that you can explore it more fully. Step into being this image. Take a breath and really feel how it is to be this image. How does it feel physically, mentally, emotionally? When you feel that you have a sense of what it's like to be this image, ask yourself the following questions:

- What are the important qualities of this image?

- What is the best thing about being you (the image)?

- What is the worst thing?

- What do you hope for as this image?

- What do you most need?

- What would you like to happen next?

- What advice do you have for 'self'?

Based on an exercise by Dina Glouberman

3.3 *(continued)*

You may find it useful to have a conversation with 'self'. Swap back and forth between being the image and being self so that you can find out more about what this image means to you and how it represents something important about you.

When you are ready, finish as 'self' and allow the image to fade. Sit quietly for a few moments and think about what the image meant for you. How does this relate to your life and what is happening for you at the moment? What were the important qualities of your image? When you are ready open your eyes and draw or write about your image.

3.4 My life path so far

Imagine that you could represent your life as a path that you've travelled along from your birth to the present day. Imagine what this path looks like. Is it smooth or does it have 'rocky' patches? Are there bridges? Ravines? Lakes? Woods? Crossroads? Take some time to draw your life path, marking on it any important events. As you draw your path, think about how you have felt physically, mentally and emotionally as you travelled.

3.4 (continued)

When you get to the present day on your life path imagine that you have reached a crossroads. Add a signpost to your drawing to show possible future paths.

Do you have an idea about what the different directions might be called?

3.5 Same and different

Although each of us is a unique individual we do, of course, have things in common with others as well. Our need to feel part of a group or community may lead us to actively seek out like-minded people. Feeling part of a group and being accepted and appreciated by a group gives us a sense of belonging and helps us to feel good about ourselves, especially when our internal reserves are low. Sometimes, however, we may find ourselves behaving in ways that don't truly reflect our self-concept in order to *appear* to fit in with a group. If you have ever found yourself in this situation you will know how uncomfortable it can feel. In the long term this can lead to a lowering of self-esteem rather than an increase.

Think of someone you know who you consider to be like-minded. What things do you have in common? How are you different?

Now think of someone else who you admire. List ten qualities that you admire in them.

Which of these admired qualities do you have?

3.6 Me, my family and my community

Where do you 'fit' with others? Imagine that the circle below represents a group of your family or friends. Who, if anyone, would you place at the centre of the circle? Where would the other people be in relation to each other and in relation to the centre? Where would you place yourself at the moment? Is this where you want to be? If not, put yourself where you would feel more comfortable.

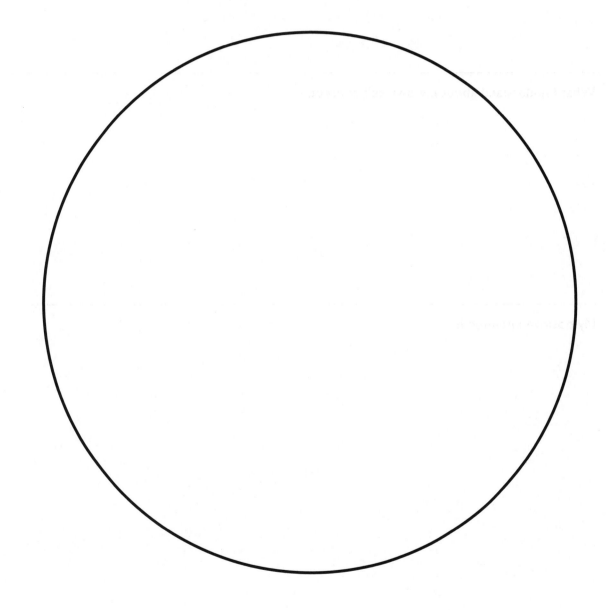

3.7 Summary

What I understand about self-concept:

What I understand about my own self-concept:

My positive intention is:

You are now going to spend some time exploring self-awareness. This includes being focused in the 'here and now' and understanding more about your own emotions.

Section 4

Self-Awareness

Being Self-Aware

Self-awareness involves being able to identify your emotions and understand the reasons why you feel the way you do in different situations. It also involves an awareness of your body and the way in which your thoughts can affect you physically.

Perhaps there have been times when you have imagined something so clearly that it has felt as though it was actually happening. This could, of course, be a pleasant experience, but you may find yourself more frequently thinking about negative things. The fear, anxiety, tension or worry that you experience at these times can feel very real. This is partly because the imagination directly affects the autonomic nervous system – that part of our nervous system that controls such things as heart rate, breathing and blood pressure. So thinking about what might go wrong in your life actually causes your body to react as though you were already facing that difficult situation: your imagination acts as a connecting system – it connects your mind, body and emotions.

Your imagination is also setting up a 'blueprint' for trouble. So if you eventually do have to face the situation in reality you already have a 'memory' of it not going well. Telling yourself how badly you are going to cope in this way may therefore lead to actual poor performance – your imagination results in a 'self-fulfilling prophecy'.

For example, if I believe that I am 'shy' or 'clumsy' then I will have images of myself in any situation acting in a 'shy' or 'clumsy' way. I will continue to expect myself to act in this way and my images will strengthen my beliefs about myself.

Fortunately, it is possible to change old image patterns and use the power of the imagination in a positive way to affect our future behaviour and thoughts. You have already started to explore this in some of the exercises you did earlier on in this course.

4.1 Focusing

Focusing involves directing your attention to different areas of your body and just being aware of any sensations. By keeping your attention on physical sensations you are training your mind to be focused in the 'here and now' rather than caught up with thoughts about the future or the past. By observing your body in this way you will also probably find that you naturally allow any areas of tension to relax and release.

You may want to make your own recording of this exercise. If you do, remember to read the instructions very slowly and calmly with plenty of pauses to allow yourself time to focus fully.

Settle yourself into a comfortable position and allow your eyes to gently close, withdrawing your attention from the outside world. Begin to notice your breathing – without trying to change anything, just noticing the natural pattern as you breathe in and out. You might notice this by being aware of the rise and fall of your stomach or you might be aware of the feel of the air as you breathe in and out through your nose.

Continue to focus on your breathing for a few moments. When other thoughts come into your mind, just acknowledge them and go back to being aware of your breathing…

Now take your attention to your feet. Focus on your feet as though you had never really thought about them before. Notice the sensations in your feet just at this moment. They may feel warm or cool, numb or tingling, painful, tense, relaxed. There is no right or wrong feeling. Whatever is there just notice it.

Now allow your attention to leave your feet and move easily and smoothly to the lower part of your legs. Notice whatever feeling is there just at this moment… Now move up to your knees and the upper half of your legs and notice whatever feeling is there… Now to your hips and lower back…and then gradually along the length of your spine… Begin to notice your shoulders, focus on all the feelings around your shoulders. Notice the back of your shoulders; across the top of your shoulders and down into your arms…

Feel what's happening in your arms… Whatever is there, just notice it… Remember there are no right or wrong feelings. Whatever you can feel is OK…

And now focus on your hands and fingers… Notice the backs of your hands… the palms of your hands…and each of your fingers in turn…

4.1 (continued)

Now the lower half of the front of your body… Move your attention along the front of your body until you reach your chest…and go a little deeper and see if you can notice your heart beat… Again, as other thoughts enter your mind just let them pass through and refocus your attention back to your body… Now to your shoulders again. Be fully aware of your shoulders… Then becoming aware of your neck – the sides of your neck, the back of your neck… Be aware of the sensations in and around your throat…

Become aware of your jaw now. Are your teeth pressed together or are they slightly apart so that your jaw is relaxed?… Notice your eyes and the sensations around your eyes… Become aware of your forehead and notice any expression on your face… Moving your attention now to the top of your head…down the back of your head…and resting once again at your shoulders…

Now instead of thinking of yourself in parts, be aware of your whole body…sensing your whole body…being aware of how sensations change from moment to moment… Continue to focus in this way for a few moments.

Now while still sensing your body, start to listen to whatever sounds there are around you… Begin to move your hands and feet a little bit… In a moment you will open your eyes. When you do, focus your gaze on one particular thing in the room and while you look at it, keep sensing your body and listening to the sounds around you… So, when you feel ready, open your eyes and look at one thing with your full concentration. Now shift your gaze to something else…and come back to the room fully, allowing other thoughts to return. You may want to stretch or shift your position.

What did I learn about myself while I was focusing?

Information sheet 4B

Awareness of Emotions

Do you place different value on different emotions? Perhaps you view some emotions as OK to have and others as not OK. Of course all feelings are real, but perhaps you are more comfortable with some than with others. If we frequently deny or 'bottle up' our feelings they may eventually feel quite uncontrollable. We may also stop trusting ourselves and our own feelings, not even certain how we should be feeling in some situations.

If we are unaware of what we feel then this will also affect how we are with other people. For example, my first feeling after a difficult encounter with someone might be 'I feel bad' but I might express this as anger. Or, if I don't feel comfortable with feelings of anger, I could end up feeling hurt and upset instead, even when anger would have been justified.

It is important to recognize all your emotions and listen to what your body is telling you. Useful, appropriate emotions brought about by realistic thoughts lead to positive action. For example, it may be appropriate to feel anxious about some situations so that you can make sure you are well-prepared in advance.

Some emotions can seem overwhelming at times and can stop us from making the changes that we want. However, by changing the way that we think about ourselves and about the situation we can often experience different or less intense emotions instead.

One way that we can help ourselves with this is to remember that other people do not control our emotions. I may feel embarrassed or fed up about something but these feelings are my reactions to situations – they can't be forced on me.

We always have choices about how we feel. This also means that we can't assume that others know what we are feeling unless we tell them. They may be able to hazard a guess but could quite easily get it wrong!

4.2 How I normally express emotions

Think about how you normally express your emotions and consider whether or not your responses are always useful/appropriate.

Emotion	How I normally express this emotion	What I experience as a consequence

Is there any specific behaviour from your list that you would like to change and could realistically alter at this stage? Look on this as an experiment. How could you alter a particular way that you express an emotion? What do you anticipate would be the result of this change?

4.3 State management

If we can 'get in a state' over something just by thinking about it, just imagine the benefits of choosing what state we'd like to be in! This really is a possibility. If we can work out exactly what a particular state of feeling is composed of then we can learn to think ourselves into that state at other times.

Every state has very specific elements:

- Body posture, muscle tension, breathing, movement

- Inner pictures, feelings, sounds and self-talk

- Our attitudes, beliefs and values that determine how we *experience* events.

Identifying the elements of a desirable state, and learning how to recall them when you want to, gives you a valuable personal resource.

For this exercise you will be asked to think of a time when you have felt particularly happy, peaceful, successful, in control or have experienced any other enjoyable 'state' of being that you would like to reproduce in other circumstances.

Choose a specific memory of a time when you were in a positive state that you would like to experience more of. Think of the exact moment that was the best part of the whole experience.

Imagine that there is a circle in front of you on the floor. This is the circle of calmness, success or whatever state you want to explore. Close your eyes and step into the circle. Imagine yourself as if you were actually in your remembered situation again. Notice the key features of this state. Really breathe into being in this state. Where exactly are you? Who is with you? How are you standing or sitting? What can you see around you? What can you hear? How do you feel? What are you thinking?

When you feel that you are experiencing it as fully as possible allow an image to come into your mind that somehow represents this state for you. Perhaps there is also a word or gesture that goes with this state? If so, say the word out loud or make the movement that shows how it is to feel like this.

Now physically step out of this state (step out of the circle). Open your eyes, talk about something else or focus your attention on something in the room.

When you are ready, step back into the circle. Use the image you came up with and/or the word or gesture that links with your positive state. This time you are aiming to experience the state without having to imagine the past event that last triggered it. Repeat steps 3 & 4 two or three times until you feel you can experience your desired state just by using your image and word or gesture.

4.3 (contunued)

When you are ready, step out of the circle again. Now think of a situation in the near future where you would like to have this positive state.

Once more step into the circle and regain your positive state. This time, imagine going into the future event while in this positive state. How do you feel? What is happening? What are you aware of? What are the new possibilities?

When you have finished this exercise, take some time to make notes about what you have experienced.

4.4 Summary

What I understand about self-awareness:

What I understand about my own self-awareness:

My positive intention is:

As you have been working through these activity sheets you will have already been making some changes. Perhaps you have begun to think differently about some situations or about yourself. Perhaps you have started to make changes in the way that you respond to some people or situations. To help you to keep these changes working for you, the next section looks at what change is all about.

The Challenge of Change

Definitions and Descriptions

Personal construct theory

American psychologist George Kelly outlined a theory of personal development which we can use to help us to understand how we make sense of the world and how we deal with change.

Kelly suggested that each of us is like a scientist: we look for patterns in how the world works, then we make hypotheses (form beliefs about the world and ourselves) and test these out by 'experimenting'. Sometimes our experiments seem to prove our hypotheses and so strengthen our belief system. At other times our experiments don't turn out the way we expected, so then we either alter our beliefs or alter our experiment. In this way we have potential for constantly 'reinventing' ourselves.

As our beliefs are formulated and strengthened, we start to predict or anticipate events. These anticipations determine what we do and think. So if we form some beliefs that are not useful to us, we may continue to act and think in ways that hold back our progress.

Imagework

Imagework is the term created by Dr Dina Glouberman to describe the methods she has developed for using imagery to understand and change our lives.

Each person's imagery is unique to him or her. It represents our own personal way of relating to ourselves and the world; our own personal way of thinking. We can use imagery to come to a better understanding of our beliefs and to formulate new beliefs that will give us more choices about how we lead our lives and enable us to create a more positive future for ourselves.

5.1 What is change?

We are all constantly changing, constantly recreating ourselves. This is inevitable. We cannot not change!

Each day we experience new situations, meet new people, hear or read new information and then we adjust our emotions, reactions, memories, storehouse of knowledge and so on.

Building self-esteem involves several changes. For example:

- changes in the way that you see yourself in difficult situations and in the way that you react in these situations

- a change in attitude about the part played by other people in the maintenance of your self-esteem

- changes that you may notice in the way others react to you as you try out more new things

- a change in your general lifestyle as you try out different and more effective ways of handling people and events

- a physical change as you alter such things as habitual muscle tension.

What are your feelings about change?

5.1 (continued)

Free Association

On a large sheet of paper write down the word 'change'. Next to this write down the first word that comes to mind that you associate with change. Now write a third word which immediately comes to mind in relation to the second, a fourth which relates to the third and so on.

Keep writing as fast as you can, putting down the first word or phrase you think of each time. Only stop when you have about ten words/ phrases or when you are starting to repeat what you have already written.

When you have completed your own free association exercise discuss this with one other person. How do your words differ from theirs? How are they alike? Have you discovered anything about how you view the process of change in your own life?

5.2 Coping with change

Think of a time in your life when you have made a change of some sort. This may have been through your own choice or through circumstances.

- What was it that you changed?
- Why did you make this change?
- How did the change happen?
- How long did it take?
- How did you feel about it?
- Was there anyone else involved?
- Did you plan beforehand?
- What happened afterwards?
- Did this change trigger any other changes?
- Was it an enjoyable change?
- Were there any surprises?
- Were there any disappointments?
- Is there anything you would like to have done differently?

Discuss this with one other person in the group. Do you have anything in common in how you cope with change?

Have you discovered anything about what you personally need to have or need to know in order to make the changes that you want?

5.3 Motivation for change

Why do people make changes? Knowing what motivates you to change can help you to make more conscious choices about the way that you change and will help in the long-term maintenance of change.

Make a list of things which might motivate you to make changes in your life such as having fun, being popular, relationships with others or personal success.

Put them in order of importance to you.

5.4 Keep it or change it?

Imagine that you could buy, sell or exchange some things about yourself. What would you buy more of? What would you sell? What would you happily exchange and what would you want to exchange it for? What would you definitely want to keep?

I would sell:

I would keep:

I would buy:

I would exchange:

5.5 Making a commitment

Write down one small thing that you would like to change.

How would making this change be of benefit to you?

Imagine that this change has already taken place. You are already benefiting from having made this change. How are you different? What is happening in your life? How do you feel? What, if anything, was difficult and how did you overcome the difficulty? What are you most pleased about with regard to this change? What will happen next?

5.6 Obstacles in the way of change

Deciding on a goal and realizing the benefits of achieving that goal are an important first step, but why is it that so many of us never get any further than this? Let's now look at the way we often resist change in our lives.

What do you consider to be 'obstacles' to change? What might prevent you from making the changes that you want?

Resisting Change

Change can be rewarding and stimulating but also daunting because of the element of the unknown. Sometimes we resist change even though we know it might be of benefit to us. In the 1950s, American psychologist George Kelly identified several possible factors that might influence this resistance. Here are four of them:

Threat is defined by Kelly as the awareness of an imminent change in our central or 'core' constructs. Our core constructs are the most resistant to change because they define the essence of how we see ourselves, and how we make sense of the world. We don't want this change to happen so we may try to avoid or sabotage change. Threat is extremely uncomfortable. You may experience the sensations associated with panic or anger.

Fear is described as an awareness of an imminent but smaller change. It is not as strong a feeling as threat but can still be fairly unpleasant!

Anxiety is experienced when we are faced with an event that has not been part of our previous experience so we can't accurately predict what is going to happen.

Guilt is experienced when we feel we are about to step or have already stepped outside the 'core' role structure we have invented for ourselves (i.e. our own standards of behaviour, not social or cultural codes).

Kelly argued that the way to overcome these feelings is to actively 'experiment' so that we can increase the range of our experiences. If we don't experiment (take action) we may try to keep our world small and manageable, avoiding changes because of fear, anxiety, guilt or perceived threat. We tend to stay with or return to what we know best so that we are able to predict outcomes (even though this may be harmful to our physical, emotional, mental or spiritual well-being). It takes an investment of time and courage to move away from this habitual pattern and to replace it with new ways of acting and thinking.

5.7 Working on avoidances

Make a list of any situations, people, feelings or relationships that you know you try to avoid.

Think about why you avoid them. What do you fear happening?

What benefits do you experience by avoiding?

Choose one thing that you are going to approach rather than avoid. What is the worst thing that could happen? How will you minimize the chances of this happening? What previous positive experience can you draw on to help you?

Desensitization

Becoming more desensitized to difficult situations is an ongoing process rather than a separate phase of building self-esteem. Desensitization in this context doesn't mean becoming 'numb' or unaware of your feelings. When self-esteem is low we may become acutely sensitive to other people's reactions to us and constantly plagued by worries about what they may think of us. Desensitization is about making realistic assessments of situations and not allowing adverse responses to worry us too much.

For example, if you feel uncomfortable in groups, when you enter a situation where you may be called on to speak you could find yourself thinking 'Should I speak or should I stay quiet?' You may then start to worry that if you do speak, others may not find what you have to say interesting. You may end up saying little or missing the opportunity to say what you wanted.

This approach/avoidance dilemma results in anxiety and physical tension. For some people, when they do speak they then blush or are very hesitant and this increases the dilemma.

We all avoid doing things from time to time, perhaps because we have no motivation for doing them or perhaps because we fear the consequences of having a go. You may have found that over the years you have built up a series of strategies to avoid certain feelings, situations or people.

Unfortunately, the more that we avoid something because we fear it, the more the fear builds up until it eventually dominates much of how we think and act.

One of the biggest steps forward in building your self-esteem is to begin to eliminate avoidance strategies. The more you face your worries head on, the more easily you will be able to cope with them.

5.8 Desensitization

What does the term 'desensitization' mean to you?

What are the benefits of becoming more desensitized to difficult situations?

List some possible ways of helping yourself to become more desensitized. Choose one thing that you will do during the next week.

5.9 Taking risks

Many of us have a fear of having to deal with rejection or failure if we attempt to make changes. We may decide not to even try, and because we don't try we will build up more and more fear about the situation through having no experience from which we can predict how things might turn out. In a sense, every change involves a risk but taking that risk reduces the fear.

Our imagination can always come up with worse scenarios than need ever happen, so once you have decided to take a risk of some sort remember to visualize a positive outcome!

Make a list of the ways in which you could lessen the possible difficulties involved in taking a risk.

5.10 The ABC of change

Sometimes the reasons for a difficulty in making or maintaining a change are not immediately obvious. The following exercise will help you to look at a problem in more depth. This method may not always help you to find the best solution but it will give you plenty to think about.

Identify the problem that you want to explore and write it down under the heading A1. It may be a decision you need to make or something you would like to change about yourself but which you are finding hard to do.

Find the opposite of this and write it down under A2. So, for example, you might write 'stay in this job' under A1 and 'actively look for another job' under A2 or 'smoker' under A1 (something you would like to change about yourself) and 'non-smoker' under A2.

Write down the disadvantages of A1. Think of as many as possible. Now list the advantages of A2.

You can now begin to look at the reasons why it might be difficult to change. Begin by finding the ADVANTAGES of A1 (your present situation). This highlights the 'payoffs' of staying as you are. Under A2 write down the DISADVANTAGES of changing.

Now look at the whole table and ask yourself: (a) Do I still want to make the change? (b) If I still want to change is there any way of achieving it without losing some of the advantages I am experiencing at the moment? Is there a way in which I can reach a compromise? How can I resolve any dilemmas that this has shown up?

The exercise that you have just done may give you an indication of why it is difficult to make certain changes. Perhaps it has given you some ideas of areas you would like to look at in more depth.

5.10 *(continued)*

A 1	A2
Disadvantages	Advantages
Advantages	Disadvantages

5.11 Summary

What I understand about the process of change:

What I understand about my own ways of coping with change:

My positive intention is:

So, you have thought about change and perhaps you are making decisions about the direction in which you want to change. You have thought a little about how you are going to begin to make these changes. This might be a good point to remind yourself that you are *already* a valuable, worthwhile person and that you are making these changes for yourself, not for anyone else. The need to be accepting of yourself and to recognize how much you are achieving along each step of the way is essential as you continue to progress.

Section 6

Self-Acceptance

The Vicious Cycle

What we believe to be true about ourselves affects the way we think. This affects how we feel and this in turn has an effect on our physical state and therefore our behaviour. The cycle can be positive or negative. Here's how it might work:

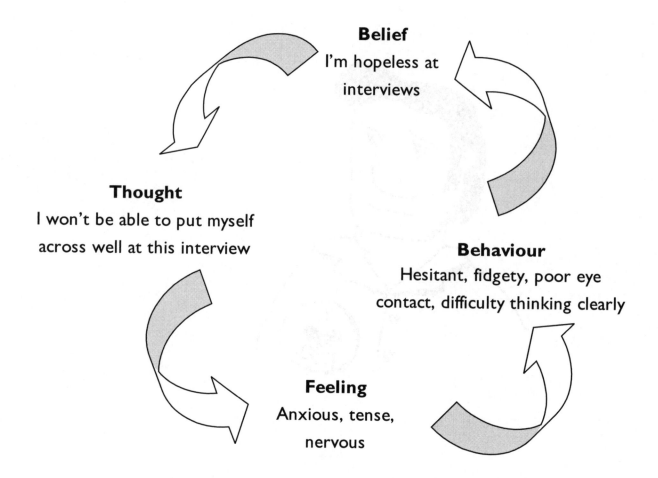

Belief
I'm hopeless at interviews

Thought
I won't be able to put myself across well at this interview

Behaviour
Hesitant, fidgety, poor eye contact, difficulty thinking clearly

Feeling
Anxious, tense, nervous

When things don't go well we can end up feeling bad about ourselves in a way that spills over into other areas of life. We might start to think 'I can't do anything well' or 'everyone else is more confident/clever/better- looking than me'. Even when new evidence presents itself that would seem to contradict our belief we deny it or make it out to be unimportant, a 'one off', a 'chance event', 'not of our doing' etc.

6.1 Challenging your beliefs

What are some of your beliefs about yourself and your life? Which of these strengthen your self-esteem? Which beliefs lower your self-esteem? How efficient is your wheel?

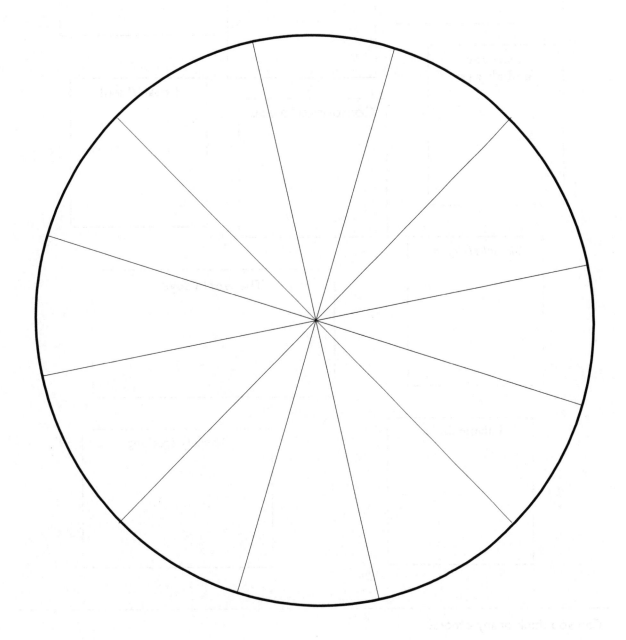

6.2 Some common patterns of self-talk that lower self-esteem

I know what
you think

These things always go
together

Total disaster

Everyone
and always

Compared to you

I should/I must

The whole of me

The world says

I blame the cat

Vaguely speaking

Can you think of any others?

6.3 Analysis of a difficult situation

My difficult situation is _____

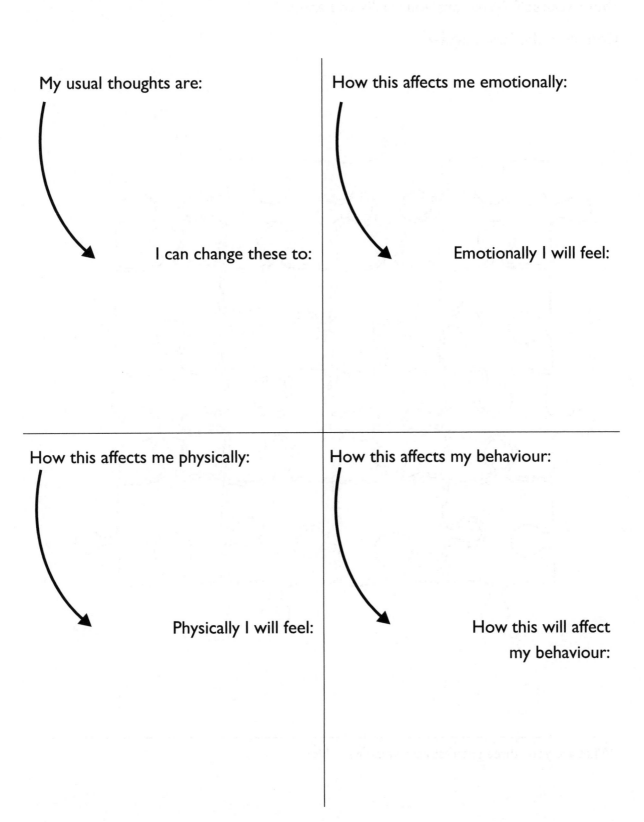

My usual thoughts are:

I can change these to:

How this affects me emotionally:

Emotionally I will feel:

How this affects me physically:

Physically I will feel:

How this affects my behaviour:

How this will affect my behaviour:

6.4 Appreciation

What would you most like other people to know about you? What do you appreciate about yourself? What are your skills and assets?

Complete the 'asset jigsaw':

What are your three greatest achievements in life?

6.5 Work in progress

What are you 'working on' at the moment that you are particularly pleased about or proud of? What would you like other people to praise you for attempting?

Write your list of work in progress inside the boulder.

6.6 Confidence

Loss or lack of self-confidence is usually experienced in relation to specific areas and for a specific reason. I can be confident in one area and not in another.

What does confidence mean to you? Think of someone well-known who you admire and who you believe to be very confident. Imagine that they are standing in front of you. What is the first thing that you notice about his or her appearance? How do you feel when you look at this person?

Now imagine that you can become this person for a few moments. Close your eyes and step into being this confident person. Allow your body posture to change so that you can really get a sense of what it's like to be very confident. What do you notice? As this person, how do you stand, walk, talk? How do you approach others? What do you think about being you? What sort of clothes do you wear? How do you make decisions? What advice do you have for others about building confidence?

It doesn't matter if you don't really know this person well enough to know the true answers to these questions. The idea is to get a strong sense of how someone might experience this level of confidence.

When you feel ready, step back into being you again. Think about what you experienced. Draw or write about the key elements of confidence as you experienced it.

6.7 Recreating a memory

Remember a time when you have felt confident in the past. Where were you? What were you doing? Who were you with? How did you know that you were feeling confident? Be as specific as you can be about how you experienced the feeling of confidence. What did you feel physically? What were your thoughts? If you can create this scene vividly enough in your mind you will be able to recreate the feeling as well.

Make a list of times when you have recognized these feelings. Add to this list when you recognize these feelings again during the next few weeks.

6.8 Summary

What I understand about self-acceptance:

What I understand about my patterns of thinking:

My positive intention is:

Self-acceptance is, of course, the foundation for secure and fulfilling relationships with others. This is the next area to consider as you build your self-esteem.

Section 7

Self and Others

Self-Esteem within a Relationship

Levels of self-esteem have a big influence on how we form and maintain relationships with others. This includes important relationships, such as with partners and close family and friends, as well as those with acquaintances, such as people we work with for a short while or meet up with while we are at school or college.

How we see ourselves will affect how we view others. If we think that people are judging us, we are likely to act in a defensive way. This could mean that we become aggressive or perhaps very passive. If we fear rejection, we may be tempted to avoid forming close relationships all together. Our behaviour will then undoubtedly affect how others behave towards us.

As with the 'vicious cycle' that we looked at earlier, this cycle of feelings and behaviour within relationships is not inevitable. When we feel strong in ourselves we tend to trust others more and we are also more discerning in who we choose to have as our friends. In turn, a person with healthy self-esteem tends to attract genuine respect and liking from others.

There is, of course, an added element here. Although we can change our own thoughts and behaviour, we cannot enforce a change on anyone else.

Changes in the way that others think and behave may occur as they adjust their perceptions of you and recognize the way that you are making changes in your life. However, this will happen at their own pace and in the context of their personal scheme of the world.

7.1 Getting a broader perspective

Think of a friendship you have had in the past that did not go as well as you would have liked, perhaps one that you felt had a negative effect on your self-esteem.

First of all think about what the other person did or said that you feel contributed to the situation not working.

Now think about what you did or said (or didn't do/didn't say) that may have contributed to the difficulty.

Imagine the person is sitting in front of you now. What would you like to say to them? What would you like to ask?

Imagine that you can become this person for a moment. As this other person, what is your perception of the situation? What do you want to say or ask?

Swap roles again and continue the conversation until you feel you have reached an understanding of some sort. What have you discovered?

7.2 Some questions for discussion

What do you think are the important elements of a secure, fulfilling relationship?

What do you feel are your 'rights' within any relationship?

What are the special qualities that you are able to offer in a relationship?

7.3 The house of relationships

Imagine that you have the address for someone who is the world expert on relationships! You have the chance to visit this expert and ask any question about relationships that has been on your mind recently.

Take a few moments to imagine yourself finding this house. Just allow it to emerge in your mind. What does it look like?

Imagine yourself standing at the entrance and remind yourself of the question that you have come to ask. When you are ready, imagine yourself entering the house. Have a look around. What is the atmosphere of this house? What are its qualities? For example, is it new or old? Does it feel busy or empty? What are your feelings now that you are here?

Somewhere in this house you will find the right expert to talk with. Have a look around until you find them. It could be someone you know, but it may not be! When you find the expert ask your question, talk with them about what is happening in your relationships.

Now imagine that you could become this expert for a moment. Step into being your expert. Take three full breaths as though you are really breathing into being this image. How do you feel? What are your strengths? What is your special quality or talent that means you are an expert on relationships? What advice do you have to give?

Continue the conversation, swapping between being 'self' and the expert until you feel that you have come to an understanding about your question. Finish as 'self'. Thank your expert and imagine yourself leaving the house. Gradually allow the images to fade from your mind and bring yourself back to the present moment.

7.3 (continued)

Make some notes or draw something that reflects your experience of this image.

What Is Assertiveness?

Assertiveness is about believing in yourself and believing that your opinions and feelings are as valuable as anyone else's and that you have the right to express them. Assertiveness does not mean always getting what you want. Instead, it may sometimes mean reaching a workable compromise.

Being assertive involves having enough self-esteem to be able to stand up for your rights without becoming aggressive.

It means being able to accept constructive criticism as well as cope with criticism that is unjustified. It is recognition of the fact that you have the right to make mistakes.

Someone who is assertive is able to give praise freely to others without feeling that it somehow devalues their own achievements. They are also able to accept honest praise and not look for hidden motives or reject it as being false. Assertiveness is about communicating clearly and confidently.

Non-assertive behaviour tends to be passive, aggressive or manipulative:

- Passive behaviour involves giving way to other people's needs, wants, opinions and feelings.

- Aggressive behaviour is about crossing other people's boundaries. This can involve such things as making decisions for other people as well as being verbally aggressive.

- Manipulative behaviour refers to actions that are aimed at trying to make someone else feel 'bad' about something or feel guilty.

These are types of *behaviour*, not types of people.

7.4 The chocolate debate

We all behave assertively sometimes, but when our self-esteem is threatened there are some common behaviour patterns that you may be able to recognize in yourself or in others. Imagine that you and some other members of a fictitious family are having a discussion about the merits (or not!) of chocolate. You will each be given a different role to play in this discussion and you will get the chance to play all the roles. When you have finished, think about the following questions:

_____

Which of the four ways of communicating was the easiest for you?

_____

Which of the four was the hardest?

_____

In your everyday life, which way of communicating do you tend to use when your self-esteem is low?

_____

What have you learned from this exercise? What decision can you make now?

7.5 Being heard

Learning specific skills related to assertiveness helps us to think more positively about ourselves and to make informed choices about what we want from life.

You may have had experiences in life that have led you to believe that your opinions and feelings are not important. If you feel this then stop and think again! Everyone has the right to be heard.

List five reasons why each of the following people should listen to you:

• Your partner/a good friend

• Your boss or someone else who has authority over you

• Someone you admire

• Your local MP

7.6 Assertive requests

There are certain strategies that can help you to remain focused and confident when you first start to experiment with assertiveness. Remember, these are only guidelines to help give you some structure.

- Think about your body language.

- Set the scene.

- Decide what you would like the outcome to be but be prepared to negotiate.

- Use 'I' statements. Take responsibility for how you are feeling.

- Be clear about the separateness between you and others. Just because someone says or does one thing doesn't mean that you have to react in a certain way.

- Be specific in your requests and ask the other person to be specific too.

- Acknowledge the other person's point of view (empathize).

- Keep an eye on your common goals.

- Stay with your statement. Avoid allowing your self-esteem to be 'hooked'.

7.7 Saying 'no'

Many people find it difficult to say 'no' to an unreasonable request without feeling guilty about it or worrying that they will lose the respect of the person who made the request. It is important to make it clear to yourself (and to the other person) that it's the request that's being rejected and not the person who made it.

If you have been asked to do something that you really don't want to do, how do you normally respond? Do you make excuses? Do you clearly state 'no'? Do you pussyfoot around and avoid making a decision? Do you end up complying with the request and feeling 'put on'?

Think about your experiences of either you
or someone else saying 'no' in an indirect way.

Again, there are some simple guidelines to help in this sort of situation. When someone makes an unreasonable request:

- Notice your immediate physical reaction and trust it. Your body will let you know whether or not you feel the request is really unreasonable (for example you may get a 'sinking' feeling).

- Give yourself plenty of time. If you notice yourself hesitating before replying then take this as a sign that you may need more information before you make a decision.

- If, after being given clear information about what the request involves, you still feel you need to say 'no' then try saying this clearly and simply without making lots of excuses. Remember to actually use the word 'no'!

- Check that your body language is also saying 'no' without looking overly apologetic or aggressive.

7.8 Coping with criticism

Listen carefully to what the person is saying. Do not interrupt with explanation or become defensive. Are you clear about the nature of the criticism? If not, ask for an example. Decide if the criticism is:

- completely valid
- partly valid
- not valid at all

If it is valid:

• State what you agree with	'Yes, I was late'
• Explain how you feel	'I feel..........about it'
• Acknowledge the possible effect of your behaviour	'Does it make things awkward for you?; I realize this must have made things awkward for you'

If it is partly valid:

• Agree with the part that is true and disagree with the rest	'You're right, I do find time-keeping difficult, but I'm not lazy'
• Say how you feel	'I'm offended that you think that'

If it is not valid at all:

• Reject it firmly	'No. I don't agree. I'm not lazy'
• Add a positive statement	'I'm very enthusiastic about this'
• Ask for clarification	'What makes you think I'm lazy?'

Finally, let it go! Don't automatically assume that a criticism means you have failed in some way. The other person is giving you feedback *from their point of view*. Look for consistent feedback from a number of people. Take responsibility for which aspects of the feedback you will act on; it is your choice whether or not to change your behaviour.

7.9 Giving feedback to someone else

Sometimes it is appropriate to give honest and clear feedback to another person when you think their behaviour is inappropriate to the situation.

Appropriate feedback is non-judgemental, clear information to the other person about how his or her behaviour affects you. Remembering the guidelines for assertive requests and assertive responses to criticism that you discussed before, what do you think would be appropriate guidelines for giving someone else feedback?

Guidelines	Examples

7.10 Giving and receiving praise and compliments

It is important for us to feel comfortable giving feedback to each other in the form of appropriate praise and compliments. This also involves being aware of 'biased scanning'! It is easy to reject compliments that have been given in all sincerity by responding with such things as 'Oh, it was nothing'; 'I wouldn't be able to do it like that again'; 'I just grabbed the first thing out of the wardrobe'. If compliments and praise are given genuinely and received openly they can act as extra 'coinage' in our self-esteem pots!

How do you praise others?

How do you feel when you are praised?

What is an assertive way of accepting praise?

How do you praise yourself?

7.11 Summary

What I understand about self-esteem within relationships:

What I understand about my own way of relating to others:

My positive intention is:

Even when we enjoy secure, fulfilling relationships with others it is important that we maintain responsibility for our own well-being. Do you respect yourself enough to take care of yourself and to ask for appropriate help when you need it? Have a look at the next set of activities. These may help you to decide whether or not you want to make changes in the way that you look after yourself.

Section 8

Self-Reliance
and Stress Management

Stress Management

If you were going to enter a sports competition or go on an arduous mountain trek you would need to be properly prepared and would take time to build your strength and stamina beforehand. Yet how often do you find yourself facing stressful situations in your life feeling unprepared, tired or simply unable to cope? When you look after yourself you are more ready to enjoy the exciting and fun things in life and more ready to cope with things that are challenging or difficult.

A certain amount of stress in our lives is useful and necessary. It is, for example, one of the factors that motivates us to achieve. It can spur us on to action and is important for success in work, sport and play. There seems to be a 'peak' of stress that we can handle – a maximum level of stress under which we can continue to function effectively. However, if our perceived stress goes beyond this level, or if stress is prolonged or managed inappropriately, it may become a problem.

The types of things that different people find stressful (their stressors) are very much dependent on personality. The ways in which you react to your stressors and develop your coping strategies are also very personal.

Effective stress management therefore involves increasing your understanding and awareness of *what* you find stressful, *why* you find it stressful and your personal *reactions* to stress. You will then have more options open to you for changing aspects of your current stress management that are no longer helpful.

As you work through the next few activities it is important to remember that we develop our coping strategies because we believe that they will help. Even some of the less beneficial ones often work for a short while. Don't be hard on yourself if you have chosen strategies that are no longer working. Ask yourself 'Why did I develop that particular strategy? What was my aim? Can I now fulfil that aim in a more positive way?'

8.1 Identification

Identifying and naming some of the things that you find stressful is an important first step.

Think of six or more situations that you find stressful. List them under the headings below. Within each category try to put them in order of most stressful to least stressful.

Daily activity/work

Relationships

Health/physical well-being

Emotional well-being

The Stress Reaction

There are several ways in which too much stress can upset a person's well-being. There are also many normal reactions that occur when we are faced with a stressful situation. These reactions prepare the body for 'flight or fight'; in other words to enable us to physically fight the oncoming threat or to run away from it. The fight/flight reaction includes the following signs:

- Your muscles tense for action. This can result in aches and pains or feeling 'shaky'.

- The heart pumps harder to get the blood to your leg and trunk muscles, ready for action. This can feel like palpitations.

- There is less blood elsewhere and so your skin might go pale and the movements of your stomach may slow down or stop (giving you a sudden 'sinking feeling' in your stomach).

- Your intestines may become more active. This gives you the sensation of butterflies or 'churning' feeling.

- Your salivary glands may dry up, causing a dry mouth or throat.

- Your breathing is likely to become faster because your lungs need to take in more oxygen more quickly and also get rid of carbon dioxide.

- You start to sweat because this stops your body from getting overheated during vigorous activity.

- Your body produces stress hormones, such as adrenaline, to keep this stress reaction going.

8.2 Physical signs

We each tend to develop certain patterns of stress reaction, with some of the flight/fight responses being more pronounced than others. For example, some people respond to stress with raised blood pressure, others with increased intestinal activity, others with increased sweating, and so on.

All these very normal responses occur because the body is preparing to face or run away from potential danger. If the reaction is completed and the 'danger' is dealt with, then the body can relax again. Unfortunately, we often produce this reaction in situations that don't actually need a physical response. These things may happen even when we are just worrying about something without resolving it, concerned about a forthcoming test, a potentially difficult conversation or being late for an important appointment. Unwanted stress reactions can also occur when the original stressful situation is no longer there but we have not done anything to ease the stress response.

What physical signs do you experience when you are under stress?

A threat to your self-esteem can sometimes have the same physical effects as if you were actually in danger and preparing to fight or run away.

Negative self-talk tends to prolong the stress response because if you tell yourself such things as 'I can't cope, it's all going wrong' your body continues to react by staying ready for action.

Recognizing the Signs of Stress

Some possible signs are:

- feeling tired/lethargic
- restlessness
- a change in sleeping patterns
- shortness of temper
- unable to 'switch off'
- weepiness
- feeling 'low'
- difficulty in concentrating
- feeling frustrated
- changes in voice quality
- feeling of tightness or a lump in the throat
- increase in hesitant speech
- constipation/diarrhoea
- difficulty in making decisions that didn't cause problems before
- feeling anxious for no particular reason
- blurred vision
- headaches
- aching muscles
- indigestion
- change in appetite – eating more/less
- an increase in reliance on alcohol, smoking or other drugs.

Some of these may occur for other reasons as well, but if you know they are stress-related then appropriate stress management can help to alleviate these symptoms.

Mark which responses you have experienced. Is there anything else you can think of that hasn't been listed?

8.3 What can you do to cope with everyday stress?

One of the first things to consider when looking at stress management is the importance of maintaining a balance between different aspects of your life.

Look at a typical day for you. Make a list of all the activities you would expect to carry out during this day and write down the approximate time each one would take.

Look carefully at this list and categorize each activity under headings such as work, study, leisure, family. Make an approximate time total for each section.

Type of activity	Time totals

Have a look at any imbalance in the list you've just made. Could you make any changes?

8.4 Enjoyment

Make a list of at least six leisure activities that you enjoy (even if you feel you don't have enough time for them).

Think about what it is that attracts you to each of these pastimes. Possible reasons might be:

Alone/with others	Funny/serious	Risky/safe
Indoors/outdoors	Competitive	Relaxing
Active/passive	Thought-provoking	Creative
Challenging/familiar	Self-development	Other

Can any of the activities that you do at the moment be altered to include more of the elements that you enjoy? Are there any new activities you would like to get involved in which would include some of these?

Make a list of 'mini ways to look after myself'. This list might include such things as going for a short walk, going to the gym, relaxing in a deep bath, phoning a friend. Try and get at least 20 items on your list. Perhaps you could decide to do one of these things every day.

8.4 (continued)

Laughter is a great stress-buster! Researchers have found that when we laugh we release 'feel good' chemicals into our body. A good 'belly laugh' or 'a fit of the giggles' may even have effects on our immune system, helping us to fight some illnesses. Fostering strong positive emotional states through humour and not taking ourselves too seriously provide an excellent boost to self-esteem.

What sorts of things make you laugh? How would you describe your sense of humour? How can you enjoy more laughter in your life?

Think about the clothes that you wear. What message do you think you give to others about the way you feel about yourself? Are you happy with this or is there anything you could change about your clothes and general 'style' to give a stronger message of 'I enjoy being me'? This doesn't need to involve a spending spree! It could be as simple as adding some colour or re-vamping some clothes that you had forgotten about.

8.5 Worry crunching

Worry involves thinking about, talking about and imagining what we *don't* want to happen in life. It is the equivalent of deliberately setting ourselves unhelpful goals!

You will probably have been aware that during long periods of worry your body reacts as though the event is actually taking place now. Most noticeably, your muscles will tense ready for action. Worrying can wear us down and sometimes leave little room for other thoughts.

Writing a worry down or telling someone else often helps to ease it straight away. Make a list of the things that you are worried about at the moment. Define them as clearly as possible. Next, sort your worries into three categories: worries you can do something about; worries that you can't do anything about because they are not personal to you; worries that are from your past that you can forget about now.

Next to each of the worries that you can do something about write a short plan of action, e.g. tell someone (specify who), be honest about saying 'no', make an appointment with the doctor, read up about it.

As soon as you make a decision to act you will find that the anxiety and tension will begin to lessen.

8.6 Procrastinating and prioritizing

If having too much to do is one of your stressors, you may find it helpful to write down everything that needs to be done and put them in order of priority.

Ask yourself 'What needs to be done today? What needs to be done by the end of this week? What could I ask someone else to do? What really doesn't need to be done at all?'

Prioritizing is not the same as procrastinating! Think about what happens when you put off doing something that you don't like doing. Perhaps it's a tricky phone call, or telling someone you can't help out or finishing a piece of work. How do you feel if you keep putting it off? Some people prefer to do things at the 'last minute'. If you don't like doing this then making an action plan and getting started on it will take away a lot of the stress involved. This will free your mind and your time for something else that you *do* enjoy doing.

Things that I tend to put off doing:

8.7 Posture

Our posture and breathing patterns, like words and gestures, can be seen as ways in which we express our thoughts. When we are stressed we may show it in the way we sit, stand and walk. Our emotions can also be expressed at a more subtle level in our muscles. For example, someone who has always suppressed his or her tears may have a permanently tense jaw. Someone who is very angry or resentful much of the time may have constantly tense shoulders.

Identifying areas of unnecessary tension and learning how to relax the muscles can increase our sense of well-being and greatly reduce the stress reaction. An upright, balanced, relaxed posture can help you to feel calm and confident.

Draw a picture or body outline of yourself and mark any areas of pain or tension that you are aware of in your body:

8.8 Breathing patterns

A calm breathing pattern is another vital factor in the management of stress. It's very easy to take our breathing for granted because it's an automatic activity and most people don't think about it on a conscious level.

If you watch a baby or young child asleep you will see the ideal breathing pattern – slow, deep and regular. Their stomach will be rising and falling easily and smoothly.

However, breathing patterns can change, sometimes for prolonged periods of time. Health problems are an obvious cause. Breathing patterns may also change as a reaction to stress.

Check your own breathing pattern. Sit in a comfortable chair or stand in front of a full-length mirror. Place one hand lightly on your chest and the other hand on your stomach. Watch what happens as you take a full breath in and then release the air slowly.

- Which hand moved the most?

- Did your shoulders rise?

- Did your stomach move in or out?

- Did your posture change in any way?

If your breathing was relaxed you will have felt your stomach expanding as you breathed in and falling as you breathed out. This movement will have been very relaxed and gentle. There will have been only slight movement in your chest. Your shoulders will have hardly moved at all. Your posture will have remained balanced.

Inspiration and Expiration

Breathing in is called inspiration or inhalation. Breathing out is called expiration or exhalation.

Inspiration involves muscle power, and the two major sets of muscles used are the diaphragm and the intercostals. The diaphragm is the large muscle under the lungs. It divides the contents of your chest and the contents of your abdomen. The intercostals are long muscles between the ribs. When your diaphragm contracts it becomes flatter and, because it is attached to the lower edge of your rib cage, this causes your chest cavity to increase in size. Air is then automatically drawn in through your mouth or nose and into your lungs. The lower ribs (called floating ribs because they are not fixed to anything at the front of your body) move outwards as your lungs fill with air. The upper ribs are fixed to the breast bone and so there is not the flexibility for much expansion of the top of the lungs. The greatest area of expansion is therefore at the base of your lungs.

Expiration does not require muscle power. As you breathe out, your muscles simply relax and your lungs return to a smaller size ready for the next in-breath. This type of relaxed breathing is called diaphragm or abdominal breathing (although all breathing involves *some* diaphragm movement).

When you are physically tense or you are anxious you are more likely to revert to upper chest breathing. This type of breathing mainly involves the top half of your lungs. As you saw earlier, upper chest breathing happens naturally as part of the stress reaction when we are under threat.

If you push air out you will be tensing your intercostal muscles and your diaphragm on the out breath. This type of forced expiration also involves muscles in the outer wall of the abdomen. These press upwards on to the bases of the lungs and force the lungs to become smaller so that air is forced out. All this extra tension increases the feelings of stress.

8.9 Using abdominal breathing for stress management

As you can see, there is a very close relationship between breathing and relaxation. If your breathing is tense then your body cannot relax completely, and if your body is tense then your breathing will not be as deep and regular as it could be. Abdominal breathing helps you to feel calm and focused.

Being aware of your breathing and training your mind to follow your breathing pattern (rather than be constantly preoccupied with other thoughts) for short periods each day can increase your feeling of general well-being and your ability to cope successfully with the stresses of daily life.

Getting started

Sit in a comfortable position, perhaps with your eyes closed so that you can focus completely on your breathing.

Start by simply being aware of your natural breathing pattern. If you are abdominal breathing already, then notice the rise and fall of your stomach. If you are upper chest breathing, then remember that the idea is to relax your stomach as much as possible.

When you have established a comfortable rhythm to your breathing continue with the process for about 15 minutes. Your thoughts are bound to wander off onto other things. This is very natural. No matter how often this happens, just notice it and then gently bring your mind back to focusing on the rise and fall of your stomach.

Take time to do this every day for a week and notice any changes in how you feel when you are doing it.

Notice what happens if you take your attention to your breathing at various moments during each day. Notice what happens if you take time to establish awareness of abdominal breathing at times when you are feeling particularly stressed.

Relaxing Your Body

Our bodies need physical relaxation in order to balance out the times when we are using our muscles in physical activity. Relaxation also involves awareness and control of signs of stress.

You will have the chance to try out several methods of relaxation. Once you have chosen the method that feels right for you, you may find it helpful to read the instructions onto a tape so that you can relax without the need to memorize them.

Your initial aims when practising relaxation might be the following:

- to learn what it feels like to be totally relaxed

- to discover any particular areas of tension in your body and to learn how to control these

- to experience a sense of control over any moments of anxiety in your life.

It is very important to keep practising. You may not experience immediate results; it may take a few weeks before you begin to feel the benefits in your daily life, but it's important that you continue to make time in your life for developing this skill.

Relaxing Effectively

There are certain conditions that will help you to relax more easily.

You will need to set aside about 30 minutes during which you know you are unlikely to be interrupted. It is important that you don't feel constrained by the time limit or feel that you need to rush to do something else as soon as you've finished. Ideally this relaxation time should be at least once a day (twice if you feel you can manage it) but not within 2 hours after any meal, since the digestive processes may interfere with the sensations of feeling relaxed.

Wear loose clothing and make sure that the room temperature feels comfortable.

Choose a comfortable position, either lying down or sitting in a chair with good back support. If you are sitting and your feet don't easily reach the floor, it's essential that you use some form of support so that you are not tensing your leg muscles.

Don't worry about whether or not you are successful in achieving a deep level of relaxation. Just allow relaxation to occur at its own pace. Expect other thoughts. When you notice these distracting thoughts just let them pass through your mind and gently go back to focusing on your chosen relaxation method.

Eventually you will notice the feelings of relaxation coming more and more easily.

When you finish, sit quietly for several minutes, at first with your eyes closed and then with your eyes open. The next thing that you do should be very calm and slow. Take your time, move gently and speak in a relaxed way so that you can keep the feeling of calmness and stability for as long as possible.

8.10 Diary notes

Note down those times when you think you will be able to spend time relaxing during the coming week. After each relaxation session make a note of how things went.

	a.m.	p.m.
Monday		
Tuesday		
Wednesday		
Thursday		
Friday		
Saturday		
Sunday		

8.11 Relaxation score sheet

Day	Time	Before	After

Give yourself a score of between 1 and 10 as to how tense you felt before and after each relaxation session. For example, a score of 1 would mean that you were very relaxed and a score of 10 would mean that you were very tense.

Do this for each type of relaxation that you try. This will help you to decide when it is the best time of day for you to practise and which type of relaxation technique is most suitable for you.

8.12 Action plan

Write down three things that you will do in order to achieve a greater degree of control in the management of stress during the next week. Be specific. For example, 'When I notice signs of stress I will go for a walk for _____ minutes; use diaphragm breathing; take some time for myself; talk to a friend.'

1.

2.

3.

8.13 Imagine a miracle

Imagine that while you are asleep tonight a miracle happens – any stresses that you are feeling at the moment completely disappear. You don't know that this miracle has happened because you are asleep, but when you wake up in the morning you feel very different.

Imagine that it is actually tomorrow morning. Think yourself into being in bed, having just woken up. Take your time to really get a sense of yourself waking up and feeling stress-free. What is the first thing you notice about the way you feel physically? How do you feel mentally? And emotionally? Imagine yourself opening your eyes. What can you see? What can you hear? How do you get out of bed? Do you get up slowly or do you leap up? How do you get ready for your day? What do you have for breakfast? What are you thinking about?

How do other people know that you feel different? What do they notice about the way that you look; about the expression on your face; about how you sound?

Do you notice anything different about other people? How do they greet you? How do they look at you?

What do you imagine happening as you go through the morning? Keep asking yourself 'What am I doing/feeling/saying/thinking/experiencing that is different?' Try and fill in as much detail as possible.

When you feel that you have a real sense of how your morning unfolds when you are stress-free, let the images fade from your mind and bring yourself back to the present moment.

Put down some thoughts about what you have just experienced.

Now here's the challenge! Is there anything you have written down that you could do tomorrow? What if you lived tomorrow morning *as if the miracle had happened*?!

8.14 Summary

What I understand about being self-reliant and the management of stress:

What I understand about my own management of stress:

My positive intention is:

When we start to manage our stress levels effectively we have more thinking space and energies left to develop other areas of our lives. The next section looks at how you can divert some of this energy into recognizing and developing your social skills and your unique way of expressing who you are.

Section 9

Self-Expression

9.1 Social skills

Sometimes feelings of low self-esteem can mean that we don't get the most from our encounters with other people because we have never learned or have forgotten the social skills that some others seem to take for granted.

These skills are needed in everyday life, to be able to communicate effectively with family, friends, neighbours, people in shops, etc., and to be effective in whatever work we choose to do.

We learn some social skills from important adults when we are growing up and we develop some through interaction with our peers. Many professionals are also offered social skills courses as part of their training (for example teachers, interviewers, salesmen, social workers). Using these skills in a more conscious way to support yourself in the changes that you are making can be very important in building and maintaining your self-esteem.

What do you think are the main skills involved in a successful social interaction?

Some skills may be relevant for use in one situation but not in another. This will depend on such things as who you are talking to and the aims of the conversation.

9.2 Pyramiding

Think of someone you know who you believe is skilled in social conversation. Imagine that you are able to observe them at a party or having a meal with some friends. What is it that they are actually doing and saying that leads you to believe that they have good social skills? In the group you will be shown how to use a 'pyramid' structure to identify specific, concrete examples of socially skilled behaviour.

9.3 Eye contact

Maintaining appropriate eye contact is one indicator of feeling comfortable in a situation. When you feel your self-esteem is threatened you may find it difficult to keep relaxed eye contact with certain people. It may feel as though the other person can 'see' your true thoughts or recognize how ill at ease you are if you allow them to look directly into your eyes. However, if you do not maintain a natural gaze you are likely to give exactly the messages that you are trying to avoid!

Who do you think does more 'looking' – the speaker or the listener?

When you are speaking, what do you feel if the other person breaks eye contact with you?

When you are listening, what do you feel if the speaker doesn't look at you?

What signals do you give to other people if you maintain relaxed eye contact?

Is there any one person or any group of people that you find it particularly difficult to keep eye contact with? Do you know why? Would you like to change this? If the answer is yes, think of one very small 'experiment' that you could make that would help you to increase your use of this skill.

9.4 Starting a conversation

A key social skill is knowing how to start a conversation in a natural relaxed way. Different people will have different ways of doing this and there really are no hard and fast rules, but once again there are some general guidelines which can help if you're feeling a bit hesitant about speaking with someone.

- Use open-ended rather than closed questions.

- Notice and respond to any new information

- Offer some information about your self and see if it's picked up.

Examples of open-ended questions:

Examples of noticing and responding to new information:

Examples of offering some information about yourself:

Do you or does anyone else in the group have other effective ways of starting a conversation?

9.5 Listening skills

If you watch good friends talking together, you will perhaps notice a very natural 'rhythm' to their conversation. It is not uncommon for people who are on each other's wave length to mirror each other's body movements. They will be talking at a similar volume and probably a similar speed. They are also likely to be using the same sort of language, responding to what the other person is saying rather than introducing completely new topics. These are signs of being in rapport. Rapport is established through skilled 'active' listening, but this can be surprisingly difficult if your own thoughts, feelings, questions and anxieties keep interfering. Such interference reduces the quality of listening and may lead to a breakdown in the communication.

What do you think are effective listening skills?

9.6 Maintaining rapport

For this next activity you will take turns with two other people to talk about something that you are particularly interested in and that you think will interest your listeners. Each of you will have a turn at being speaker, listener and observer. When you are the listener use the 'active' listening skills that you have already identified. Your aim is not just to listen to the words but really to try and understand what the speaker is thinking, feeling and meaning. The observer's task is to watch and listen and give feedback to the listener on which skills they have used. You can use the checklist that you made as a reminder. When you have discussed the exercise in your small group take some time to answer the following questions for yourself.

What elements of effective listening do you already use?

How do you *show* others that you are listening?

What percentage of a conversation would you normally listen for?

Are there any changes that you would like to make to your listening skills?

9.7 Pausing

You've already discussed the fact that effective communication is not just about speaking a lot, but most of us will have come across at least one person who, once they get started talking, doesn't seem to pause for breath! Pausing is important for a variety of reasons.

Why do we pause?

Do you think you use pauses appropriately? Are you able to tolerate silences within a conversation? Would you like to change anything about the way you use pauses?

How will you monitor any changes that you make?

9.8 Ending a conversation

What might be some of the difficulties involved in bringing a conversation to a close? Think about face-to-face interactions and telephone conversations.

If you want to finish a conversation, but the other person sounds as if they could keep going for the next couple of hours, what do you normally do or say? Is this effective?

How would you move on from one group to another when you are socializing with lots of people? Is this effective?

Do you or does anyone else in the group have ways of bringing a conversation to a close in a way that leaves everyone feeling OK about it?

9.9 Imagine it again!

Remember a time when you have been in a situation where you have spoken confidently and had an enjoyable conversation with someone. Imagine yourself being in that situation again.

- What do you sound like?
- What do you look like?
- What does your body feel like?
- What are you thinking?
- What can you see?

This is what happens when I am speaking confidently:

My breathing is	My posture is
My speech is	I feel
My thoughts during speech are	My thoughts after speaking are

9.10 Summary

What I understand about social skills:

What I understand about the way that I express myself:

My positive intention is:

While you have been identifying areas for change you have also been trying out different methods for solving potential or actual problems. Seeing problems as opportunities for progress and development and being able to find creative solutions can be a tremendous boost to self-esteem. So, how creative are you? Are you ready to invest some time s in exploring this aspect of your abilities?

Creative Problem-Solving

Creative Problem-Solving

The same method of problem-solving may not necessarily work for different situations and different types of problem. This is why it is important to develop creativity in dealing with difficulties.

We all have creative potential but many of us fail to use it constructively. The amount of creativity we use is closely related to our self-concept. Do you think of yourself as a creative individual or as a creature of habit? Do you tend to be quite logical and methodical or, when appropriate, can you make use of a more holistic, overall view of a problem and use intuitive ideas?

By trying out new methods of problem solving we can begin to tap into the wealth of creativity that our minds are capable of. This can be effective even in times of extreme difficulties. If we believe that we are capable of finding a way through even seemingly insurmountable problems then we are much more likely to be experimental in dealing with difficulties. As we experience successes, we start to trust our judgements and decisions more and more. This helps to confirm our abilities and self-worth and gives us confidence to know that we will be able to cope with future difficulties effectively. This, in turn, allows us to have more patience with ourselves, with others and with life.

So each time you solve a problem in a new way you are developing your creative potential and this can have big payoffs, rather like depositing money in a high interest savings account! Even obstacles and setbacks can provide creative opportunities if you can learn something from them.

Take some time to think how you normally go about problem-solving. In your group you will discuss a range of difficulties that might require different approaches. Write down some ways in which you would start to generate ideas about these difficulties.

In this exercise you are not looking at the ideas themselves but just methods of coming up with creative solutions. For example, do you normally write lists of pros and cons for different ideas? Do you have 'brainstorming' sessions with other people? Do you meditate? There is no right or wrong answer, just see what you can come up with.

10.1 How do you normally set about solving problems?

(a)

(b)

(c)

(d)

(e)

In doing this exercise, you have probably come up with several different ways of problem-solving. You may have found that you often use methods involving logic and reasoning. For most people, logical thought is primarily a left brain process. In contrast, the right side of the brain is concerned with such things as imagery, recognition, creativity and intuition. In the right hemisphere mode of thinking, people describe 'moments of insight', that 'aha' sensation when things suddenly seem to fall into place and we 'get the picture'. Being aware of our ability to use both the left and the right halves of the brain when faced with difficulties means that we have a wider range of choices available to us and a greater possibility of fulfilling our potential.

10.2 What skills are involved in problem-solving?

See if you can 'solve' these problems:

- Can you tie a knot in a piece of string without letting go of either end?

- Can you draw a dot inside a circle without taking your pen off the paper?

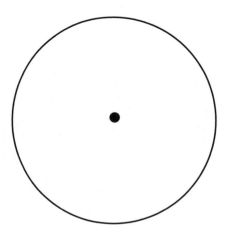

When you have worked out how to do these two tasks, take some time to think about the skills involved and make a list.

10.3 Problem focused or solution focused?

Problem-solving is about focusing on possible solutions rather than dwelling on the problem itself. Perhaps there has been a time recently when you have solved or reduced a problem. What did you do? How did you arrive at a solution? What steps did you take? Be as precise as possible in recalling the details of this. Think about your thought processes, your feelings and your actions. What worked? What didn't work? What did you learn from the experience?

The problem was:

I felt:

The way I thought about it was:

My decision was:

10.3 (continued)

My first step was:

_____

Then I:

_____

The outcome was:

_____

I felt:

_____

What I learned from the experience:

10.4 More examples

Here are some more examples of methods of problem-solving. Try them out for yourself and see what works best for you.

- Sit quietly on your own for 20–30 minutes and just let your thoughts flow freely. Very often, towards the end of this period you will suddenly gain insight into the difficulty that you are 'mulling over'.

- Divert your energies into something physical, such as going for a walk. Again, you will often find that a solution comes to mind when you are least expecting it.

- You may have found that you had sudden flashes of inspiration when you were practising relaxation. The more deeply relaxed you are in both mind and body, the more likely this is to happen.

- Sit with a pencil and paper and write down the problem in the form of a question. For example, 'How can I make the best use of my time today?' Now write all the possible solutions that you can think of. Write down anything at all which you think might help, even if it would be difficult. Try to get at least 15–20 answers. Sometimes the last few answers are the most useful because you have had to think beyond the more usual ideas.

- Brainstorm ideas with a group of people. Take at least 30 minutes for this and ask one person to be the 'scribe'. Everyone shouts out ideas for the scribe to write down on a large piece of paper. Do not discuss the ideas as they come up or in any way judge their merit, even if they seem wild or impossible. The object of the exercise is to get as many solutions as possible from varied perspectives. These can be sifted through at the end in order to select the best options.

- Instead of seeing the difficulty as something to be sorted out or eradicated, try using positive language and change it into a challenge rather than a problem. Decide how you would set about working on this challenge and use your goal-setting skills to systematically work towards achieving the most appropriate outcome.

This sort of creative thinking can be very energizing, spurring us forward into action!

10.5 Using imagery

(Based on an exercise by Dina Glouberman)

Think of a difficulty that you are currently working on. Sit quietly for a few minutes and let yourself gradually relax. Allow your eyes gently to close.

Invite an image to come into your mind that represents the difficulty. It might be an image of an animal, an object or a plant. Just allow whatever comes to mind, no matter how strange or ordinary it might seem.

Now examine the image very closely. Look at where it is, notice its relationship to its environment. Is it alone or are there other things around it? How does it look from all angles; from in front and behind, from above and below? Does this image move or make sounds? If it could talk, what would it want to say to you? Find out as much as you can about this image, remembering that it represents your present difficulty. What is its history? Has it always been like this or was there a time when it was different?

Now imagine that it is some time in the future and that your difficulty has been resolved. How does your first image alter? Do not force it to change, just let things happen. Again, look at its environment, examine it from all angles. Is there anything there that you hadn't noticed before? What is the next step for this image? Where would it most like to be? If it needs to change any more, how will it change? Imagine this change taking place as you watch.

When you are ready, allow the image to fade and gradually become more aware of your present surroundings. Take your time over this and as you become more alert remain sitting quietly and see if you can 'map' your image onto your actual difficulty. How does the image relate to the problem to be solved? How do the alterations in your image relate to possible solutions? Sometimes the answer is clear, sometimes you will need to bring the image to mind over a period of days to make sense of it.

10.6 Using drawing

(adapted from an exercise devised by Tom Ravenette)

In a similar way to using visual images in our minds, drawing can also be used to look at different aspects of a problem and to create links between present and future. Using drawing as a method of problem-solving may give you added insight to a situation.

Sit quietly for a moment and choose a difficulty that you are working on. When you have chosen something just let it sit in your mind – don't try and consciously work out a solution. Using the line below as a starting point, draw a picture that fills the rest of the page. Don't think too deeply about it and don't worry about 'getting it right'; just allow the drawing to emerge. Remember, fill the whole space; don't restrict yourself to one object but think about the background as well.

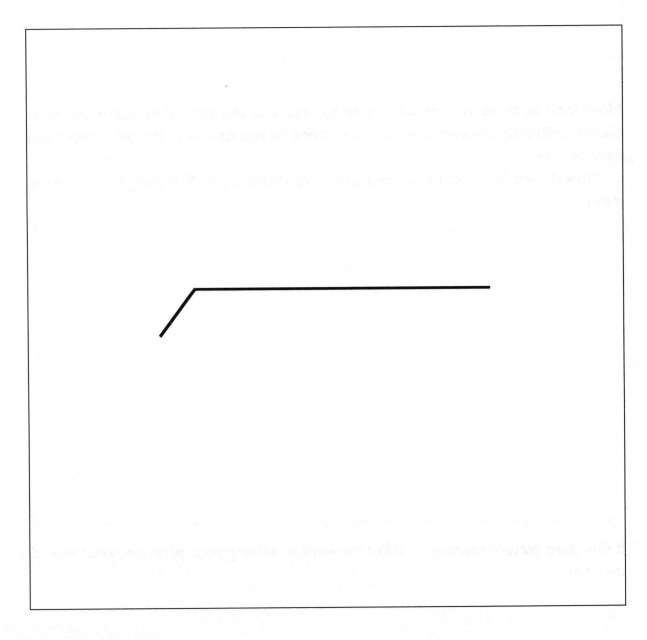

10.6 (continued)

When you are satisfied that your drawing is complete, look at it carefully and then draw a second picture which in some way represents the opposite of the first.

Now look at these two pictures side by side and see how they represent your dilemma/difficulty/concerns. What associations do you have with the two images you have drawn?

Now draw a third picture. Draw anything you want to; the first thing that comes to mind.

If this third picture represents different ways of solving your problem, what would they be?

10.6 (continued)

Sometimes the solution to a difficulty does not involve an opposite extreme. For example, if I am feeling overwhelmed in a very demanding job I might feel that I would be happier in a job with little or no responsibility. However, it may be that the skill I need to cultivate is assertiveness so that I can say 'no' to unreasonable demands on my time and be ready to delegate tasks to other people. In the exercise you have just done, the third picture represents some creative alternatives for you to consider beyond that which may seem more obvious at first.

A second exercise involving drawing is to simply sit with your question in mind and begin to make marks on the paper. If you are normally right handed, try using your left hand for this. Use different colours and draw without an end product in mind. It need not look like any particular object but will in some way represent how you view the situation or how you are feeling. When you have finished give your picture a name. Now add something 'surprising' to your picture. Once again consider how this relates to your question and whether or not it gives you an indication of how you feel things might progress.

There will always be more than one solution to any problem. Creative thinking helps us to find the way forward that is most appropriate for our individual needs at the time. It enables us to have choices. Choice leads to a feeling of control and to higher self-esteem.

10.7 Summary

What I understand about creative problem-solving:

What I understand about my own methods of problem-solving:

My positive intention is:

As you are beginning to make more conscious choices and changes in your life, it will perhaps have become increasingly clear to you just how important it is to set regular, achievable goals for yourself. This doesn't necessarily come naturally to many people – it is another skill that can be developed through practice. The following section outlines some methods for deciding on and implementing your goals.

Section 11

Setting and Achieving Goals

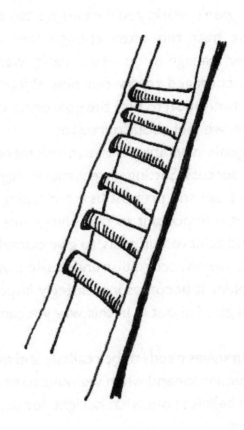

© Deborah Plummer 2005

237

Setting and Achieving Goals

The ability to set realistic and yet challenging goals is an important but often undervalued skill. Like any other skill, it takes practice and dedication.

If you look back to the section on change you will remember that you discussed how difficult change can be and some of the reasons for this. Setting specific goals helps us to be in control of the direction of change and once again contributes to the maintenance of healthy self-esteem.

Fear of failure may prevent us from formulating goals for ourselves on a regular basis. Sometimes we are told that we won't achieve our goals – that's just 'pie in the sky'; don't be silly – that won't work; you'll never be tall enough/rich enough/brave enough to do that. If we hear this often enough then it may become our own self-limiting belief ('I never manage to do what I really want').

Sometimes we are encouraged to try out new things but we are unsuccessful because we have no real motivation to fulfil the goal or no clear idea of how achieving the goal would affect how we feel about ourselves.

Setting and achieving goals inevitably involves an element of risk – we risk making a mistake but we also risk success. Setting unrealistically high goals for ourselves may make the risks seem too huge and prevent us from taking the first steps.

For all these reasons it is important to take things one step at a time and, as we begin to make changes and achieve our goals, to give ourselves a 'pat on the back'. As young children we rely heavily on recognition and praise from the important people in our lives, but as we get older it becomes increasingly important for us to recognize our own success and feel good about it. In this way we can build a stronger sense of self-worth.

So, each goal we set ourselves needs to be realistic and manageable. We need to be clear about what we are aiming for and when we want to have achieved it by. Each goal should fit in with our own beliefs about what is 'right' for us, and we need to recognize the benefits of achieving it.

11.1 If I wasn't waiting

Take two minutes to sit with one other person and complete the sentence 'If I wasn't waiting I would…' (wash the car, write a book, learn to swim, etc.) as many times as possible. This is a fast exercise. Don't think about it in too much depth. Some important things may occur to you during this exercise. Spend a few moments afterwards writing all or some of them down. Perhaps they will form the starting point for you setting yourself more regular goals.

Now ask yourself what exactly you are waiting for – more time, more money, more freedom, more confidence, more energy? Ask yourself if you really *need* to wait any longer for all the things you listed.

11.2 Guiding principles

The goals that we set for ourselves need to fit in with our view of ourselves and the world. We all have 'guiding principles' that inform our thoughts and actions. These are very central to who we are, and we are only likely to alter them if we have conclusive evidence that they are no longer valid or useful. What do you think are some of your guiding principles in life? You could think of these as 'unspoken rules' – things that you feel are 'taken as read'. These often involve words such as everyone, always, wrong, should and must. For example, some 'rules' might be 'It's wrong to show your emotions'; 'You should always think of others first'; 'Everyone has the right to work.'

When you are deciding on your goals you may find it helpful to ask yourself 'If I achieved this would I really want it?' If you have any doubts then you have another choice: do you want to alter your goal or do you want to rethink any of your 'guiding principles' that may no longer be valid or useful?

11.3 An example of using imagery for goal-setting

Have a large sheet of paper and some coloured pencils near you.

Sit quietly for a few minutes and let yourself relax as fully as possible. Gradually close your eyes. Allow your imagination to come up with an image for the following question: 'Where am I in my life right now?' This might be an image of an animal, a plant or an object. Just allow whatever comes to mind.

Now, in your mind, examine the image very closely, then when you are ready, open your eyes and sketch the image on your piece of paper.

When you have finished, sit quietly again with your eyes closed. Breathe deeply and relax. Allow an image to emerge for the question 'What is my next step?' Explore whatever image comes to you. When you are ready, open your eyes and draw the image.

Repeat this process for the following two questions:

- What is getting in my way/holding me back?

- What quality do I need to develop in order to get me through this block?

When you have drawn the fourth picture take some time to think about how these images relate to your questions. You might find it helpful to talk to someone about what you have drawn in order to clarify what it all represents. Remember though that no one else can interpret your images for you. They are very personal and will trigger your own unique associations. Only you know what significance they have.

11.4 Taking steps

Some undertakings can seem huge when looked at as a whole, but when they are broken down into smaller steps they can become much more manageable.

Think of something that you would like to achieve in the next few weeks. State your intention as clearly as possible; for example, 'By the end of this month I will be going to the gym twice a week, every Monday and Thursday evening', or 'By Friday of next week I will have given a short talk about science fiction films to the youth group and it will have gone well.'

Imagine that there is a 'time line' on the floor in front of you. This line stretches from the present moment to the time when you have completed your chosen goal successfully.

Stand at the starting point of this imaginary line and take a few moments to get a sense of what you feel about this goal. What do you feel physically? Emotionally? Mentally?

Step off the line and look at the end point. Remind yourself of your positive intention.

Walk to the end point (without walking along the imaginary line!).

Stand at the end point of the line and imagine that you have successfully completed your goal. Take as much time as you need to really get a sense of how it is to have achieved your goal. What do you feel physically? Mentally? Emotionally?

When you feel ready, take a step back along the line to a time just before you completed the goal (it could be a few minutes or hours before, or the day before). What are you doing to prepare yourself for completing the goal? What are you feeling? What's happening around you? What are you particularly pleased about?

Now take another step back along the line to a point when something different is happening, perhaps a couple of days before completing the task. What are you doing? What are you feeling? Is anyone else helping you in this task? What are you pleased about? What is difficult? What is easy? Continue back along the line, stopping at different stages and asking yourself these questions until you reach your starting point again.

Take a moment to look along the line and remind yourself what you learned and what you experienced along the way.

Step off the line. Bring yourself fully back to the present moment by saying something about how you are feeling right now (calm, tired, excited etc.) and how you know that you feel that way (my hands are tingling; my breathing is slow; and so on).

11.4 (continued)

Draw your time line and mark on it the different steps (smaller 'sub-goals') that led up to completion of your final goal. Remember that these sub-goals need to be flexible. Maybe you will find that you can miss out a stage or add an extra one or slightly change the order. Whatever you decide you will probably find that this exercise has helped you to see whether or not your goal is realistic and achievable within the time frame you have set yourself. Looking back as though it had already happened can be a great boost to your confidence. Making a note of the steps you took along the way can help as a reminder for future goals.

11.5 Being effective

Goals can be made for every area of our lives — at work, school or college, at home, within our family, amongst friends. They can be goals for things we want to achieve for ourselves or for others. We need to set ourselves a mixture of long term, medium term and short term goals.

Being effective means producing the results that you want in life, so it's important to choose goals that feel 'right' for you. There are some simple questions you can ask yourself that will help you to choose effectively.

Remember the imagery exercise you did in the section 'What Is Self-Esteem'? Here's a reminder:

Read through the following instructions or have someone read them to you. When you are ready, close your eyes and relax your body. Imagine that it is the end of the situation you chose. Imagine that things did not go well. Ask yourself the following questions:

- What did I do that meant this didn't work well?

- What was I thinking before and during the situation?

- What did I say/not say that meant this didn't go well?

- What was I feeling physically before and during the situation?

- What else do I notice about what happened?

- What is the uncomfortable feeling right now? What is the main thing that makes me feel like this?

- What was the main decision or attitude that got me here?

Now let that image go. Give your body a bit of a shake and then settle back into a relaxed position again. Remember, you are imagining that the event has already happened. This time you are feeling good because things went really well. Ask yourself the following questions:

- Exactly what are the 'good' feelings that I have now?

- What did I personally do that meant that this worked well? What did I do before the situation and during the situation that led to such a positive outcome?

- What was I thinking before and during the situation?

- What did I say/not say?

- How was I feeling?

- What else do I notice about what happened?

11.5 (continued)

So, the important points are that:

- you don't just explore what you *don't* want – you try to be as clear as possible in working out what it is that you *do* want

- you identify the specific things that *you* will do or say in order to achieve this

- you identify any evidence that confirms your success. For example, if your goal is to feel more confident with a particular group of people, you could judge your achievement by saying more than normal or by being in the group without feeling physical symptoms of anxiety.

Just one last point. You may decide at the end of this that your original goal doesn't really feel right for you any more. Sometimes when we can see what the possible outcome could be, we might decide that it isn't as great as we thought and actually we need to change it slightly (or a lot!). As long as our reasons for altering the goal are based on sound judgement and not on anxiety, we can simply go through the process again with our altered perspectives and work out what is right for us.

Have a go now at defining a goal for yourself and going through the imagery exercise. When you have finished, write down the key points that you decide on.

11.6 Summary

What I understand about the process of setting goals:

What I understand about my own goal-setting:

My positive intention is:

As you build a healthy level of self-esteem you will be increasingly able to cope with temporary setbacks and still maintain a sense of well-being. In the final part of this course you will have the opportunity to review what you have learned and to decide what action you will take to sustain the changes that you are making.

Keeping It All Going!

12.1 A review of beliefs, thoughts and actions

Helpful	Unhelpful
Make sure you have a mixture of long-, medium- and short-term goals for yourself. Make sure these are realistic and achievable.	Set unrealistic targets for yourself.
Make sure that self-praise is unqualified (That was a difficult situation and I handled it well).	Use qualifiers when self-praising (I handled that well. Why can't I always do that?).
Notice times when you are feeling OK, however brief or lengthy.	Only give attention to how you are feeling when there is a 'problem'.
Notice small achievements and comment positively to yourself: *how* do you know that you have done something well?	Only notice your big achievements. Be vague about how you know that you've done something well.
Be precise in describing your aim (While I am talking to Alan I will keep my shoulders relaxed and concentrate on listening to what he is saying).	Be vague or too general about your desired behaviour (I need to be more confident).
When self-evaluating, use non-judgemental words like 'difficult' and 'easy'.	Use 'labels' about yourself such as 'shy', 'clumsy', 'useless'. Use judgemental words to describe your behaviour like 'terrible'.

12.1 (continued)

Helpful	Unhelpful
Use 'I' statements (I feel upset).	Use 'they' statements (they're always making me upset).
Acknowledge the feelings behind your actions. Work out how you might have behaved differently in response to the same feeling.	Deny or make light of your feelings. Tell yourself that you can't change the way you react to difficult people and situations.
Be clear and consistent about your boundaries and your beliefs.	Be inflexible about personal 'rules' that are no longer useful (I have to wait for someone else to suggest an evening out).
Recognize your current abilities and be prepared to set yourself challenges and take small risks.	Be over-protective of yourself (I can't speak to that new person because I would feel uncomfortable). Be over-critical of yourself (I never have anything interesting to say to anyone).
Aim for imaginative problem-solving.	Blame yourself. Make the problem out to be unimportant.
Be honest with yourself. Be prepared to admit your own mistakes.	Avoid confronting your mistakes.
Use positives ('keep eye contact').	Use negatives ('don't look away').

12.2 Sustaining the changes

In taking responsibility for building your self-esteem you have made the most important step in achieving your goals. You have been able to look at where you are in life and where you want to be in the way that any scientist might begin to look at a difficulty to be solved. You, the scientist, now have the chance to continue to experiment. You may find that you need to reform some of your hypotheses because they are no longer valid, but that can lead to very positive changes.

Even when we know what we want to do, that doesn't necessarily mean that we will remember to do it! You may want to use as many different self-prompts as you can come up with. Think about how you already remind yourself to do things. What works best for you? Could you use any ideas that other people have come up with?

What self-prompts
am I using
successfully?

12.3 Coping with setbacks

You will be able to maintain your progress if you truly believe that what you are doing is relevant, that you are capable of doing it and that the end results are worth the effort.

You are, of course, likely to continue to come across difficult situations. Temporary setbacks may occur but, having strengthened your self-esteem, you will find it easier to learn from the experience and move on. Remember, if you can't change the situation then you will find that thinking about that situation in a different way can help you to come up with an effective coping strategy. This in turn will have a positive effect on your confidence.

For example, you may find that some people still react to you as though you had not changed. Or they may remark on your increased confidence but still be expecting you to revert to your old ways. They may continue to assume responsibility for things that you now feel capable of doing for yourself. Many people have found their progress unwittingly hampered by well-meaning friends and relatives. This will not happen, however, if you can maintain an assertive response to any attempts to draw you back into your old habits.

Devise an assertive response to a friend who has made a decision on your behalf:

Gradually, most people will adapt to the new you, and if you share your adventures and changes with them you will help them to feel included rather than excluded.

12.4 What works for you?

Write down ten things that you will do in order to feel more in control of your life. Be as inventive as you can. Write them down quickly without taking too long to think about them.

1.

2.

3.

4.

5.

6.

7.

8.

9.

10.

Discuss your list with one other person. Now add five more things that you will do.

1.

2.

3.

4.

5.

Resolve to start one of these things today!

12.5 Feeling inspired?

Collect (or invent!) ten motivational sayings that really appeal to you.

1.

2.

3.

4.

5.

6.

7.

8.

9.

10.

12.6 Letter from the expert

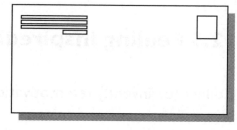

Perhaps you have made quite a few changes in the way that you think about yourself and others during this course.

Imagine yourself at the start of the course. Can you remember what you felt like and what your expectations were?

Knowing all that you know now and recognizing the progress that you have made, imagine that you are writing a letter of advice to yourself – things that you would like to remind yourself about in the future. Write anything that comes to mind. Make it as long or as brief as you want.

Put the letter in an envelope and seal it. Address it to yourself! Perhaps it will be just the thing to give you a boost at some point in the future!

12.7 Finishing the course

What are your feelings as you come to the end of your course? What do you feel confident about? What would you like to know more about?

What do you feel you have achieved during this course?

What obstacle(s) have you already overcome?

What do you think are the most important objectives for you in the future?

Appendix A

Relaxation Exercises

1. Progressive relaxation

The technique of tensing and relaxing different muscle groups and noticing the different sensations was developed by American Edmund Jacobsen in the 1930s and is still widely used (Jacobsen 1938). For full benefit this is best done lying down with your arms resting by your sides.

Make yourself comfortable and close your eyes. Spend a few moments just listening to your breathing and feeling the air go in and out of your body…in and out like waves on the sea shore… You're going to feel what it's like to tighten up different parts of your body and then to relax.

When you are ready, very gradually curl your toes so that you can feel them getting tight or tense…hold that tightness for a moment…and let go. Feel the difference between what it was like to be tense and what it's like to be relaxed… Now do that again…curl your toes…feel the tension…and let go.

Now, keeping your heels on the ground, bend both your feet up towards your head. Feel the tightness in your legs when you do this… Hold it…and let go… Feel the difference… Do that once more.

Now think about the top half of your legs…tighten the muscles in the top half of your legs so that you are slightly pushing yourself up from the floor or bed… Really feel the tension… Now relax… Do that once more… Let all the tension flow out. Your legs will roll outwards when they are relaxed. Check how this feels. Notice the difference between what it feels like when your muscles are tense and when they are relaxed. Your legs will begin to feel warm and heavy.

Now think about your back. Slightly arch your back away from the floor or bed… Hold still…and then relax… Do that once more.

Tighten your stomach muscles by pulling your stomach in towards your back… Again hold this for a moment…and then gently let go with a sigh… Now push your stomach muscles outwards. Check how this feels… Let go… Repeat this once more – first pulling your stomach in…relaxing…and then pushing your stomach outwards…and relaxing again. Make sure that your legs and feet haven't tensed up again while you've been doing this.

Now you're going to move to your hands and arms. Stretch your arms out and feel which muscles you are using…hold them stiff for a moment…now let those muscles go floppy and heavy… Do that once more… Now gently curl your fingers until you can feel the tightness…let go and feel the difference… Now stretch your fingers out and see how that feels… Do both of those things again, curling and stretching your fingers… Let your hands rest lightly by your side now. All the tightness has gone and your arms and hands feel warm and heavy.

Think about your shoulders. Very gradually and gently raise your shoulders towards your ears. Feel what that's like… See if you feel more tightness on one side than the other…let go gently… Now let go even more than you thought you could… Do this once more… Raise your shoulders towards your ears…hold the tightness…and let go…and now let go even more.

Now think about your neck. Slowly and gently drop your head towards one shoulder, just far enough to feel the pull of the muscles on the other side… Now slowly move your head back to the middle…and now over to the other side. Feel the tension in your muscles…and now gently back to the middle again. Check that you feel comfortable. If not, try doing that again.

Now gently close your back teeth together. Hold them closed very lightly…and let go. Press your lips together firmly and then let go… Press your tongue against the roof of your mouth and again let go… Your tongue is now resting on the floor of your mouth, your teeth are slightly apart and your lips are resting lightly together.

Think about your eyes. Close your eyes even more tightly than they already are… Now let go again… Feel the difference. Raise your eyebrows as though you were surprised…let go… Now frown and feel which muscles you are using…and relax.

Now wrinkle your nose…and let go.

Now instead of thinking of yourself in parts, feel your whole body relaxing, sinking into the floor. With each breath you are breathing out the tightness and breathing in relaxation. Feel the breath go in through your nose, down through your windpipe and into your lungs. Feel it filling your lungs… Feel your breath as the air leaves your lungs and travels out through your nose. Just notice your breathing for a while. Let it happen naturally but feel the flow of air. With each breath out you will feel more relaxed…and more calm… You will feel warm and perhaps a little sleepy. If thoughts enter your head, just let them pass through, then go back to feeling your breathing. Notice how your body feels different now. Enjoy this feeling for a few minutes.

When you are ready gently start to move your fingers and toes… Very gently rock from side to side just a little bit… Have a yawn and a stretch… Open your eyes gently and get used to the room again… Bend your knees and roll over onto your side before slowly sitting up.

2. Focusing

This type of relaxation works by focusing the mind on different areas of the body and just being aware of what that area of the body feels like. It is a version of the focusing exercise (activity sheet 4.1). It can be done lying down or seated. Quite often if we try to relax, we try too hard! In our efforts to relax we actually set up more tension. By observing what the body is doing there is a natural tendency to simply allow any areas of tension to relax and release. This is an exercise commonly taught as part of mindfulness meditation. It is a good exercise to do when you find your thoughts getting caught up in worries, plans and concerns.

Let your eyes close gently and settle yourself into a comfortable position. Think about your right foot and just notice what it feels like. It might be warm or cold. It might be numb or itchy. Just notice whatever you can feel…

Now think about the lower part of your right leg. Let your attention leave your right foot and just move very easily to your right leg. Notice whatever feeling is there just at this moment…

Now move up to your knee and the upper half of your right leg and notice whatever feeling is there…

Now to your right hand. Feel what's happening in your right hand…

Now think about the lower part of your right arm and feel what's happening there… Whatever is there, just notice it…

Now do the same with the upper part of your right arm. Remember there are no right or wrong feelings. Whatever you can feel is OK…

Go across your body now to the upper part of your left arm…

Now down through your elbow to the lower half of your left arm…

And now your left hand and fingers…

Now the upper half of your left leg, notice whatever is happening there…

And the lower half of your left leg…

And now down into your left foot…

Now notice both your legs and both your feet at the same time…

Now your arms and hands as well as your legs and feet…

Start to listen to whatever sounds there are around you…

When you feel ready, open your eyes and look around you. Lie or sit quietly for a short while before stretching and slowly getting up.

3. A 'calm down' relaxation

This is adapted from an exercise by Jane Madders, physiotherapist and teacher of health education and relaxation training. In panic situations, breathing tends to become shallow and fast. If you can learn to take charge early on and bring your breathing back under your control this will help you to regain a feeling of calm more easily. For this quick relaxation to be effective you should already have experienced more detailed methods.

As soon as you notice yourself getting tense or worried, say to yourself 'Calm down'. That means telling your body to stop worrying.

Focus on your hands as you breathe in (this doesn't have to be a big deep breath, just normal breathing) and, as you breathe out very slowly, allow your hands to relax. On the next breath focus on your shoulders and as you breathe out allow your shoulders to relax. Finally focus on your jaw and allow your jaw to relax as you slowly breathe out. After two or three more calm breaths continue what you were doing.

Breath Control Exercises

1. Energizing breath

- Sit upright in a high-backed chair so that your body is well supported and relaxed.

- Breathe naturally for a while, just feeling the rhythm of your breath.

- After a few breaths, press your left nostril closed with your thumb and inhale through your right nostril. Keep the natural rhythm of your breath.

- Release your thumb; close your right nostril with your forefinger and exhale through your left nostril.

- Without changing fingers, inhale through your left nostril.

- Change fingers. Exhale through the right nostril.

- Inhale through the right and exhale through the left and so on. Repeat the whole sequence ten times.

2. Extending exhalation

- Sit erect and well supported; your chest and head in a straight line; shoulders slightly back; hands resting easily in your lap.

- Inhale slowly as you silently count to three (one…and…two…and…three). Remember to breathe from your diaphragm.

- Hold for the count of three.

- Exhale slowly through your nostrils, counting to six.

- Count to three again before inhaling.

- Continue for about three minutes.

The reason for making the outbreath longer than the inbreath is that breathing in involves muscle contraction and the heart and metabolism speed up slightly. Breathing out involves relaxation of the muscles and the heart and metabolism slow down slightly. The duration of the outbreath can be slowly increased as you practise this until you are exhaling for the count of 15 or more. The important thing is to feel the rhythm rather than to try and increase the capacity too far.

3. Combining breath control and imagery

Sit comfortably in an upright position.

Imagine that you are the yolk inside an egg and that between the yolk and the egg are seven other layers. As you breathe in, imagine that you are breathing up the back of your body from the ankles to the top of your head. Pause for the count of three. Then as you breathe out, breathe down the front of your body, sweeping under your feet. Repeat this six more times, remembering the next time you breathe in to imagine that you have moved slightly further away from your body into the next level so that when you reach the seventh inbreath you are sweeping a wide circle around your body. Really let go each time you breathe out, releasing the tension from your body. Take your time with this. There is no need to rush it.

Now the next time you breathe in, breathe up the right side of your body from the feet to the top of your head and down the left hand side of your body as you breathe out. Again, do this in a circular movement sweeping under your feet and moving away from your body in a circle that gets bigger and bigger with each breath. Do this for seven breaths, remembering to pause after breathing in each time.

References

California Task Force to Promote Self-Esteem and Personal and Social Responsibility (1990) *Toward a State of Self-esteem.* Sacramento: California State Department of Education.

Casement, P. (1990) *Further Learning from the Patient: The Analytic Space and Process.* London: Tavistock/Routledge.

Eliot, L. (1999) *What's Going on in There? How the Brain and Mind Develop in the First Five Years of Life.* New York: Bantam.

Glouberman, D. (1992) *Life Choices and Life Changes Through Imagework.* London: Aquarian.

Glouberman, D. (2003) *Life Choices, Life Changes: Develop Your Personal Vision with Imagework.* London: Hodder and Stoughton.

Harper, J.F. and Marshall, E. (1991) 'Adolescents' problems and their relationship to self-esteem.' *Adolescence 26*, 799–807.

Harter, S. (1999) *The Construction of the Self.* New York: Guilford Press.

Jacobsen, E. (1938) *Progressive Relaxation.* Chicago: University of Chicago Press.

Johnson, R.A. (1989) *Inner Work: Using Dreams and Active Imagination for Personal Growth.* New York: HarperSanFrancisco.

Jung, C.G. (ed) (1978) *Man and His Symbols.* London: Pan Books (Picador edition).

Jung, C.G. (1990) Foreword in E. Neumann *Depth Psychology and a New Ethic.* Boston and Shaftesbury: Shamhala. (Original work published 1949.)

Kelly, G.A. (1955) *The Psychology of Personal Constructs.* New York: Norton.

Markova, D. (1996) *The Open Mind: Exploring the 6 Patterns of Natural Intelligence.* Berkeley, CA: Conari Press.

Maslow, A.H. (1954) *Motivation and Personality.* New York: Harper and Row

Maslow, A.H. (1962) *Toward a Psychology of Being.* Princeton, NJ: Van Nostrand.

Moore, T. (ed) (1990) *The Essential James Hillman: A Blue Fire.* London: Routledge.

Moore, T. (1996) *Care of the Soul: How to Add Depth and Meaning to Your Everyday Life.* London: Piatkus.

Overholser, J.C., Adams, D.M., Lehnert, K.L. and Brinkman, D.C. (1995) 'Self-esteem deficits and suicidal tendencies among adolescents.' *Journal of the American Academy of Child and Adolescent Psychiatry 34*, 7, 919–928.

Rayner, E. (1993) *Human Development: An Introduction to the Psychodynamics of Growth, Maturity and Ageing.* London: Routledge.

Rogers, C. (1961) *On Becoming a Person: A Therapist's View of Psychotherapy.* London: Constable.

Rogers, C. (1969) *Freedom to Learn: A View of What Education Might Become.* Columbus, OH: Merrill.

Satir, V. (1991) *Peoplemaking.* London: Souvenir Press.

Stevens, J.O. (1989) *Awareness.* London: Eden Grove.

Storr, A. (1989) *Solitude.* London: Fontana.

Zukav, G. (1991) *The Seat of the Soul.* London: Rider.

Contacts

Deborah Plummer runs training courses and seminars on self-esteem. For further information contact:

Deborah Plummer
PO Box 7485
Leicester LE3 1ZL

For information about courses and workshops in imagework visit the Imagework Association website: http://www.imagework.co.uk

General Index

activity sheets, guidelines 10, 56
avoidance 27, 77
autonomic nervous system 30–31

beliefs 14, 15, 27, 64, 79
    self-limiting 19, 31, 79

California Task Force 16
Casement, P. 15
change 16, 20
    difficulties 26–8
    framework 24–6
    resistance to 77
Communication
    see also feedback
    guidelines 47 59–60
    non-verbal 14–15
    patterns 86–8

Dalton, P. 78
depression 16
Dunnett, G 78

EEG research 15
Einstein, Albert 98
Eliot, L. 15
emotions 66, 73

feedback
    see also communication
    giving 36, 30
    receiving 39

focusing 72, 92–3

Glouberman, D. 29, 31, 32, 33, 50, 56, 63, 69, 70, 85, 100
goal-setting 19, 103
groups
    advantages 40
    beginning phase 48
    checking-in 38, 49–50
    closing circles 48, 50–51
    disadvantages 40–41
    facilitating 44–7
    follow-ups 52

guidelines 47
middles and ends 51–2
organizing 41–2
planning form 54
role models 48
structure 42–4
warm-ups 47

Harper, J.F. 16
Harter, S. 14
hierarchy of needs 17–18
    see also Maslow
Hillman, J. 33

ideal self 14
imagery 30, 58 see also images
    creating a memory 103
    de-roling 87
    facilitating 56–7, 63–4
images 29–30
    see also imagery
    creating 31–2, 57
    example 65
    exploring 69
    interpreting 33, 66
    negative patterning 34
    types 30
Imagework 28, 32–4, 37, 38, 70, 75
imagination 30
    active 32
information sheets
    use of 10, 56, 58
intentions 67

Johnson, R. 30, 32
Jung, C. 31, 32

Kelly, G. 24, 26, 27, 68

learning process 37–8
learning styles 41, 45

Marshall, E. 16
Maslow, Abraham 17, 19
    see also hierarchy of needs; self-actualization
mind
    conscious 29, 30
    unconscious 29, 30, 31, 74

mind-body interaction 30, 31, 34, 74, 80
Moore, T. 33

Overholser, J.C. 16

personal construct theory 24, 58
    anxiety 27
    constructs 25–6, 75
    elaboration 25–6
    fear 27
    guilt 27
    links with imagework 28, 75
    self-characterization 68–9
    threat 26–7

Ravenette, T. 101
Rayner, E. 17, 98
Rogers, C. 19, 37, 46

Satir, V. 9, 14, 19, 42, 85, 86
self-actualization 18, 19
    see also Maslow
self-concept 13–14, 70
self-disclosure 45
self-esteem
    see also self-worth
    assertiveness 85–6
    in adolescence 16–17, 70, 73
    benefits 4, 15, 19–20, 36, 64–5
    in childhood 14–15, 84–5
    and competency 13, 14, 15
    effects when low 19
    foundation elements 9–10
    self-acceptance 21
    self-awareness 22–3
    self-confidence 19, 22
    self-expression 22
    self-knowledge 20
    self and others 19, 20, 21
    self-reliance 19, 21–2
    global 14, 62
    and hierarchy of needs 18
    loss of 15
    and reaction to stress 91

Activities Index

Information Sheet Index